WILLIAM BARNES Poems selected by ANDREW MOTION

William Barnes was born in 1801 near Sturminster Newton in Dorset, of a farming family. He learned Greek, Latin and music, taught himself wood-engraving, and in 1823 became a school-master in Mere. He was deeply interested in grammar and language, and waged a lifelong campaign to rid English of classical and foreign influences. He was ordained in 1848. Among his best-known books of poetry are *Poems of Rural Life in the Dorset Dialect* (1844) and *Hwomely Rhymes* (1859); his work was greatly admired by Thomas Hardy, Tennyson and Hopkins. His work has often been praised for its evocations of Dorset life, landscape and customs; he also wrote political poems of great power and was a master elegist. Barnes died in 1886.

Andrew Motion was born in 1952 and educated at University College, Oxford. As poet and biographer he has received many prizes and awards, including the Whitbread Prize for Biography and the Dylan Thomas Award. He is Professor of Creative Writing at the Royal Holloway, University of London, and was appointed Poet Laureate in 1999.

WILLIAM BARNES

Poems selected by ANDREW MOTION

faber and faber

First published in 2007
by Faber and Faber Limited
The Bindery, 51 Hatton Garden
London ECIN 8HN

Photoset by RefineCatch Ltd, Bungay, Suffolk
Printed and bound by CPI Group (UK) Ltd, Croydon, CR0 4YY

A CIP record for this book
is available from the British Library

ISBN 978–0–571–23665–7

FSC
www.fsc.org
MIX
Paper | Supporting
responsible forestry
FSC® C013604

Printed and bound in the UK on FSC® certified paper in line with our continuing
commitment to ethical business practices, sustainability and the environment.
For further information see faber.co.uk/environmental-policy

10 9 8 7 6 5 4 3

Contents

POEMS IN NATIONAL ENGLISH
(Originally from *Poems Partly of Rural Life in National English*, 1846; *Poems of Rural Life in Common English*, 1868; and manuscript)

Introduction

William Barnes (1801–1886) is a major lyric poet and much neglected. It's easy to see why. Most of his poems are written in a
Dorset dialect which looks bewildering on the page and puts
people off. Several of his earliest and best-known admirers realized
this, and did what they could to give reassurances. Francis Kilvert
called him 'a great idyllic poet'. Tennyson cited him as an influence
on 'The Northern Farmer'. Hopkins called him 'a perfect artist and
of most spontaneous inspiration'. Thomas Hardy was his friend
and elegist, and introduced a selection of his work. In the years
immediately following Barnes's death there were signs that these
recommendations might do the trick. The 1879 collected edition
of his dialect poetry was reprinted four times before the end of the
century, and the *Saturday Review* said in its unsigned obituary:
'There is no doubt that [Barnes] is the best pastoral poet we pos-
sess, the most sincere, the most genuine, the most Theocritan; and
that the dialect is but a very thin veil hiding from us some of the
most delicate and finished verse written in our time'.

Since then, famous voices have continued to speak up for
him. Ralph Vaughan Williams set 'Linden Lea'. Geoffrey
Grigson compiled and introduced an edition of his work.
W. H. Auden said, 'I cannot enjoy one poem by Shelley and am
delighted by every line of William Barnes.' Philip Larkin
referred to him as 'one of the most scrupulous metrists, [and]
vowel and consonant balancers in our tongue'.

None of these golden opinions has had much popularizing
effect – and neither has Bernard Jones's two-volume edition
of the poems, published in 1962, nor a handful of subsequent
selections. Year by year, Barnes has been pushed to the side
of the English tradition, waiting for a change to occur in our
attitude to vernacular writing so that we might see and hear his
genius for the thing it is.

Dialect is not the only obstacle. Barnes further increased
the likelihood of his own neglect by resisting categories – as

Hardy acknowledged when he called him 'probably the most interesting link between the present and past forms of rural life that England possesses.' Barnes spent most of his writing life as a Victorian, yet his attitudes to Nature linked him to the Romantics: to Wordsworth, obviously, but in idiom and emphasis also to Burns, Clare and Crabbe. (The poems in his first dialect collection were divided into seasons, like Clare's *Shepherd's Calendar* of 1827.) At the same time, traces of Augustanism survived in Barnes's standard English writing. Everything about him was at odds with his own time, even his appearance: he could be seen strolling round Dorchester in the late 1870s wearing buckle shoes and knee breeches, wielding a staff. His aim was a kind of heroic individualism, a style of living and writing which set him at an angle to his contemporaries.

Much of the inspiration for this came from Barnes's childhood. He was born at Rush-Hay, by Bagber Common, two miles west of Sturminister Newton in the Vale of Blackmore, Dorset. His grandfather had inherited but been forced to sell a small farm of his own; his father John described himself in a Population Return compiled during the year of William's birth as a 'labourer in husbandry', and raised his family in an atmosphere which mingled restraint with anxiety.

In 1806, when Barnes was five, he was sent to live with his father's sister Ann and her husband Charles Rabbetts (or Roberts), who farmed nearby at Pentridge in the Vale of Blackmore, on land which ran down to the River Stour. This big clay valley, extending south and east of Sherborne, in an arc west of Shaftesbury and up beyond the Somerset border, had changed very little by the time Hardy came to remember it almost a century later in *Tess of the D'Urbervilles* (1891):

> The traveller from the coast, who, after plodding northward for a score of miles over calcareous downs and corn-lands, suddenly reaches the verge of one of these escarpments, is surprised and delighted to behold, extended like a map

beneath him, a country differing absolutely from that which he has passed through. Behind him the hills are open, the sun blazes down upon fields so large as to give an unenclosed character to the landscape, the lanes are white, the hedges low and plashed, the atmosphere colourless. Here, in the valley, the world seems to be constructed upon a smaller and more delicate scale; the fields are mere paddocks, so reduced that from this height their hedgerows appear a network of dark green threads overspreading the paler green of the grass. The atmosphere beneath is languorous, and is so tinged with azure that what artists call the middle distance partakes also of that hue, while the horizon beyond is of the deepest ultramarine.

Barnes later recalled his life with the Rabbetts and their family (they had eight children of their own) in many poems, notably 'Uncle an' Aunt' and 'Rustic Childhood'. Yet while the world they depict is compactly detailed, it has an air of remoteness about it. Barnes had scarcely finished his schooling (at a Church of England endowed school in Sturminster Newton) when the Vale of Blackmore fell victim to the agricultural depression which ravaged Dorset in the years following the Napoleonic wars. Charles Rabbetts went bankrupt, and the farm was sold. 'The young men were in reckless mood,' Barnes wrote later, 'the girls bewildered. Then were driven away the cows ... then went the wagon in which the merry haymakers had so many times ridden to the feast of harvest-home; in short everything that was dear from familiarity was taken away.' He associated the disaster with the plight of his father and grandfather, and began to idealize the remoter past of the place even more wholeheartedly.

At the same time, Barnes rebelled against his misfortune. He had excelled at school and, soon after his thirteenth birthday, he started working as a clerk for a solicitor in Sturminster Newton. In 1818 he moved to Dorchester, where he got a similar job with Thomas Coombs and Son. In the evenings after work, he studied the classics with a local priest, drew, played music, and learned how to engrave on wood and paper. 'It was always in my mind', he said later, 'that I would try to rise to a higher standing than that to which my father had fallen.'

For a while Barnes toyed with the idea of making his living as an engraver. He did some work for a bookseller in Weymouth and sent specimen drawings to a fine art dealer in London. He was told there was no vacancy. He tried again, submitting work to Edward Scriven, a London bookseller, and got the same answer. Reluctantly he accepted that his hopes of 'following a career in art' would have to be redefined. (A watercolour self-portrait he painted when a young man shows an easy but unexceptional talent, as do the two hundred or so engravings he cut over the years to illustrate technical, linguistic and architectural pamphlets.)

Just as Barnes was trying to get work in London he discovered a reason for wanting to stay in Dorchester. In the summer of 1819, when he was eighteen, he noticed a family clambering down from the stage coach outside the King's Arms Hotel in High Street East. Many years later Barnes's daughter would say that her father immediately 'found his heart . . . awakened [as] a slight elegant child of about sixteen, sprang easily down with a bright smile. She had blue eyes, and wavy brown hair [and] the unbidden thought came into his mind, "that shall be my wife".' This 'child' was Julia Miles, and she was fourteen, not sixteen years old. Her father James, a Supervisor of Excises who had previously lived in Saffron Walden in Essex, was understandably keen to shield her, and parried Barnes's first advances. For his pains, he was transformed by Barnes into a domestic tyrant. In 1820 Barnes published a small collection of clumsy *Poetical Pieces* – in standard English – which are remarkable chiefly for their hostile accounts of fathers who value money more than affection:

> Her father he lik'd the pecun'ary ore,
> Insomuch that in one of his passions he swore
> That Julia should ne'er again enter his door
> If to him she her hand should impart.

Two years later the same complaints reappear in 'Orra: A Lapland Tale' (a narrative poem influenced by Ambrose Philips's 'A Lapland Lovesong', which Barnes had read in the *Spectator*). While singing 'the sorrows of a faithful pair' Barnes reprimands those who prefer 'A life of luxury and splendour', spurns the idea that 'young love could not brook/ The woes that from poverty spring', and dismisses the adage that 'gold's the best passport thro' life'.

In 1823 Barnes accepted that if he was going to marry Julia he would have to conform to her father's expectations and find a respectable job. This led him to take on the headmastership of the Market House School in Mere, ten miles north of Shaftesbury, and before leaving Dorchester he applied once more to James Miles. He was again rejected. '[My father] told me plainly,' Julia reported, 'that he had no objection to you in the least . . . But then he told me I must remember that when you first walked with me I was but a mere child and it was his duty as an affectionate father to make objections.'

Mere was bleak compared to Dorchester. In the year Barnes arrived, its population was only 2,500, it had no public systems of lighting or water or sewage, and disease was rife among the people and livestock. None of this prevented Barnes from improving his lot – becoming, in Larkin's phrase, 'a kind of successful Jude Fawley' – but it was a lonely process. During his first five years at Mere, he and Julia only saw each other occasionally (at first in Dorchester, then in Nailsea, Somerset, after the Miles family moved there in 1825), and the letters they exchanged were kindly but guarded. As their editor says: 'A natural pedagogue, [Barnes] gave [Julia] lessons in perspective and reproves her for writing crooked-backed Ds. He never mentions her errors, but frequently correctly uses the misspelled word or incorrect name in the next letter.'

Market House School was a modest, one-roomed stone building in Mere's central square; every evening its desks were cleared away and it was used as the town's theatre. During the twelve years of Barnes's headmastership, the number of pupils never rose above two dozen, and the diet of their learning remained constant: 'Reading, English Grammar, at three guineas per annum; and if required Drawing, Music and Latin at three guineas per annum.' What this meant in practice was an education based on the formulas laid out in Locke's *Essay on Education* (1752). The *Essay* was touched with the idealism Barnes had already shown in his other walks of life, yet it also emphasized the virtues of pragmatism and self-help. Practising what he preached, Barnes spent his evenings continuing the studies he had begun at Dorchester. He investigated ancient British history. He rapidly developed an interest in languages, learning French from a Frenchman who had settled in Mere, and also studying Persian and Welsh. His education, his daughter Lucy said later, 'could have been nothing but elementary [but] this was of little importance, for the learning which made his name was no grammar school knowledge . . . No school teaching gave him his faculty of penetrating to the root of every study which came his way, it was the natural instinct of a keen and penetrative mind.'

By the spring of 1827 Barnes's school was securely based, and he was able to think of living more comfortably. He rented the large and beautiful Chantry House in the centre of Mere, overlooking the church, and immediately wrote again to James Miles asking for permission to marry Julia. Judging by the terms of his letter, recent experience in Mere had turned a defiant young man into a soberly self-confident adult. 'I have always,' he said to Miles, 'been taught to rely on my own exertions and this has brought all my powers into action and given me a greater variety of resources than those who have always followed one pursuit.' This time Miles needed no cajoling: Barnes and Julia were married in Nailsea on 9 July 1827, eight years after they had first met.

With his wife to help him, and a roomy house at his disposal, Barnes was able to take in boarders as well as day-pupils. The school flourished, increasing its range of courses as Barnes's own studies embraced new areas of knowledge, yet remained faithful to his original ideals. Trevor Hearl, one of his biographers, tells us: 'The keystone of education at Chantry House' combined Locke's principles with 'moral training based on the Christian gospels' – and Barnes was also 'deeply influenced by the [great figures of the] Enlightenment . . . whose ideal [in education] was to speak fluent French, write Italian poetry, admire Greek culture; to pen emotion in verse, have music and art at the fingertips, and reveal a knowledgeable enthusiasm for classical learning.' Barnes was renowned, too, for the kindness he showed his charges. 'During his thirty-nine years as a schoolmaster he was never known to strike a pupil or speak harshly to one.'

In the same year that he married, Barnes began contributing to the local weekly paper, the *Dorset County Chronicle*, a stoutly conservative broadsheet. He submitted prose essays to start with, but was soon sending poems in both dialect and standard English – as he continued to do throughout his life. (He also wrote for the *Gentleman's Magazine*, *Fraser's Magazine*, *The Reader* and *Macmillan's Magazine*.) His first three articles were entitled 'Linguiana' and initialled 'W.B.'. After that he branched out; eventually his topics ranged from the means by which language should be classified, to the attractions of going to auctions.

Barnes's success as a journalist, combining with the good reputation of his school and his exceptional happiness at home with his wife and children, gave his life the stability it had lacked since leaving Pentridge. Yet as his family grew he needed to earn more money, and this meant taking in more pupils. He found Mere 'out of the way', and in 1835, when he heard of 'an opening for a boarding school at Dorchester', he took it. He stayed for the next twenty-seven years. 'I put my hopes of afterlife in work at [Dorchester]' he said, modifying still further the attitude he had once taken to 'gold'.

Barnes's first school was in Durngate Street, which after two successful years he said was too small. In 1837 he moved to Norman House in South Street. In both places he kept faith with the principles he had already tried and tested: 'preparing middle-class children for the professions, the army or navy or ... the universities'. He also continued to produce a steady stream of poems – in what he called 'national' English, and in Dorset dialect as well. A first collection of dialect work appeared in 1844 with a fifty-page dissertation on his ideas about language, and a 1,500-word glossary; another, in 'national' English, in 1846; a second dialect collection in 1862; and another in standard English in 1868. In addition, he persevered with his essays for the *Dorset County Chronicle* and elsewhere. He read extensively in the large library belonging to John Richmond, the former headmaster of Dorchester's grammar school. He was also 'so lucky as to find ... a friend who was a good Oriental scholar, Colonel Besant, theretofor of the Bengal Infantry and author of the *Persian and Urdu Letterwriter*, with whom for some years [he] read a little Hindustani or Persian once almost every week'. He compiled large-scale grammatical works, including *The Elements of English Grammar* (1842) and *A Philological Grammar* (1853), which demonstrates in its 320 pages that Barnes had a competent understanding of no fewer than sixty-five languages. He also published *A Grammar of the Dorset Dialect* (1863) and *A Glossary of the Dorset Dialect* (1886).

Despite the breadth of his learning, Barnes lived between strict boundaries. He visited London only a handful of times – once to meet the poet Caroline Norton, an admirer of his own work; once to visit the Great Exhibition. His single trip abroad was to France in 1845. Yet it was a packed existence. As well as teaching and writing, he studied throughout the 1830s and most of the 1840s for a Bachelor's Degree of Divinity at Cambridge – a course which required him to spend three full terms in college. In 1845 he helped to found the Dorset County Museum. In 1847 he was ordained at Salisbury and became pastor at Whitcombe near Dorchester.

These demands were matched by dramas in his personal life. In May 1837 his only son Julius died, aged three months. Three years later a friend he had known since childhood, Edward Fuller, also died – and was elegized in the poem 'The Music o' the Dead'. When his wife Julia died on 21 June 1852, nine days after her forty-seventh birthday, from an 'ulcer' of the breast, his world was even more profoundly shaken. 'Oh! Day of over-whelming woe!' he wrote in his diary. 'That which I greatly dreaded has come upon me. God has withdrawn from me his choicest world gift. Who can measure the greatness, the vastness of my loss? I am undone. Lord have mercy upon me!'

Barnes took charge of his five children and at the same time tried to maintain standards in his classroom. Even with Julia beside him, his daily work had become increasingly difficult during the late 1840s. Now that he was alone, he made unrea-sonable demands on his oldest children and on himself ('I took in my sadness to constant work' he said) – especially after the death in 1853 of his mother-in-law, who had lived with him and Julia for the last twenty years, and had also helped in the school. No matter how hard he worked to augment his income by pub-lishing, lecturing and giving public readings of his work, his livelihood steadily ebbed away from him. At the beginning of the summer term 1859 his daughter Laura 'went into the school to find her father sitting alone at his desk with not a single pupil. He remarked gravely: "You see, I am at my post." '

Barnes persevered for another three years, reminded by his own failure of the disappointments that his grandfather, father, uncle and aunt had once endured. The struggle took its toll. The formerly 'alert and vigorous teacher' became increasingly eccentric, growing a long grey beard and, when teaching, wear-ing a 'long light-blue, rough-faced, flannel-textured dressing gown'. As his biographer Alan Chedzoy says, it was a way of advertising that he had 'ceased to live emotionally in the world he actually inhabited'.

Barnes's school eventually closed in 1862, teaching him a difficult lesson about 'the mockery' of life: on the very day he shut up shop, *The Times* announced that one of his former pupils had come first in the Indian Civil Service examination;

it brought him a flood of applications. Soon afterwards, however, his prospects brightened again: the government gave him a Literary Pension of £70 a year, and he was offered the living of Winterborne Came, two miles south of Dorchester. He was sixty-one years old, but still full of energy – walking long distances every day as he carried out his pastoral duties, continuing to develop the County Museum in Dorchester, and in 1875 founding the Dorset Field Club.

As Barnes settled into his new home – a thatched, shaggy-browed rectory – Coventry Patmore eulogized his second dialect collection in *Macmillan's Magazine*, brushing aside questions of linguistic difficulty. 'Mr Barnes,' Patmore wrote, 'is not only one of the few living poets of England, but ... in one respect he stands out in a remarkable way from other living English poets ... Seldom before has the precept "Look in thy heart and write" been followed with such integrity and simplicity; and seldom before have rural nature and humanity in its simpler aspects been expressed in verse with fidelity so charming. We breathe the morning air while we are reading.' This article not only confirmed Barnes as a local celebrity, it turned him, briefly, into a national figure. His books sold steadily if not spectacularly. He became an object of curiosity and a port of call for passing worthies, including Tennyson. Like Hardy, he was credited with the power to articulate the spirit of 'Wessex'.

Barnes lived the last part of his life quietly. To some, his reserve seemed to show a 'morbid' form of modesty; to others he appeared 'deficient in determination and spirit'. His admirers realized that he looked picturesque but intended to be practical. Hardy, for instance, admitted that Barnes was 'quaintly attired', but also knew that he 'warble[ed] his nature wood-notes with a watchful eye on the predetermined score'.

Patmore sensed the same element of calculation when he made his last visit to Winterborne Came in September 1886: 'I found him,' he said, in bed in his study with his face turned to the window, where the light came streaming in through flowering plants, his brown books on all sides of him, save one, the wall behind him being hung with old green tapestries. He had a scarlet bedgown on, a kind of soft biretta of dark red wool on his head, from which his long white hair escaped onto the pillow. His grey beard has grown very long upon his breast. His complexion . . . has become bleached by keeping indoors, and is now waxily white where it is not waxily pink. The blue eyes were half shut, restless under languid lids; the whole body was very restless, rousing and falling in bed by means of a very gorgeous bedrope, with an action like rowing a boat. I wish I could paint for you the strange effect of this old, old man, lying in cardinal scarlet in his white bed, the only bright point in the gloom of all these books. You must think I make too much of these outer signs, but it seemed to me that this unconsciously theatrical *mise-en-scène* in the solitude of this out-of-the-way rectory was very curious and characteristic.

Two months later, on Thursday 7 October, Barnes died; four days after that he was buried in the churchyard of Winterborne Came. In his elegy, 'The Last Signal', Hardy tells us that as he set out from Max Gate for the funeral half a mile away across the fields, the sun flashed off the coffin-lid, which was made of polished elm: 'Thus a farewell to me he signalled on his grave-way,' Hardy wrote, 'As with a wave of his hand.' Tennyson felt a similarly personal loss. He wrote to Barnes's daughter: 'Your father seems to me one of the men most to be honoured and revered in our day.'

*

Rescuing Barnes from obscurity means showing his weaknesses as well as his strengths; he is a poet who needs some apologies, as well as apologists. His religious conviction, for instance, can seem sentimental and smug. He moralizes too easily on the basis of Nature's example. He can seem unduly trustful of authority ('Let other vo'k meake money vaster/ I don't dread a peevish measter'). He is inclined to endorse a culture in which outcasts are pitied but not protected, and opportunities for self-help – which he preached earnestly in the classroom – are neglected. But if we allow these things to persuade us that he was someone who unthinkingly preferred the past to the present, and brought no artifice to his art, we would fall foul of the danger that Hardy warned about, and succumb to 'the popular impression of him as the naif and rude bard'. Barnes's religion may be too secure for some tastes, and his liking for the status quo too uncritical for others, but his imagination is contradictory and perturbing, and his views about versification and language all combine innocence with cunning. Hardy was right again when he said Barnes 'really belonged to the literary school of such poets as Tennyson, Gray and Collins, rather than to that of the old unpremeditating singers'.

Barnes's 'cunning' is easy to establish: many of his homely-seeming structures are in fact exotic imports. A Persian verse form is used in 'Woke Hill', Hebrew in 'White an' Blue' and 'Melhill Feast' – and elsewhere he borrows from Norse, Irish and Welsh. The same goes for his dialect itself. When E. M. Forster, for instance, said that 'the veil of the Dorset dialect . . . is slight: anyone can lift it after half an hour's reading', he meant to recommend Barnes, but in fact made him seem a much less conscious artist than was the case. Regional dialect, as a written form, had largely disappeared from books published in Britain within a century of Chaucer's death: to pretend that Barnes is not an anomaly is to play down the extent to which his work is deliberately provocative.

When Barnes published his first dialect collection in 1844, his claim to be using a 'real' language was evidently far-fetched. In the years following, it became increasingly obvious that he was not so much maintaining a distinct local tradition as using his skills as a philologist, historian and archaeologist to create a language that appeared to be common to all Dorset but was in reality his own. He spruced up the spellings in his dialect work as successive editions appeared. He demanded that 'foreign' words be excluded from ordinary speech and that Anglo-Saxon alternatives be provided. He ornamented his Dorset research with references to the Welsh language. In nearly every respect, Barnes's efforts led him further and further into oddity – and today most philologists agree that both his linguistic principles and his vocabulary were substantially of his own invention. The evidence is everywhere. Among his many other theories we find the idea of 'hard-', 'dead-' and 'half-pennings', which refer to varieties of vocal stops and chords. (The word 'penning' is not even in his own Glossary, let alone the *OED*.) Elsewhere he speaks of 'wordheads' (initials), 'lessening meanings' (diminutives), and 'clippings' (consonants). And in his *Outline of English Speech Craft* (1878) we find him offering a host of substitutes for familiar existing words: 'skysill' (for 'horizon'), 'mind-glee' (for 'delight'), 'song-mocking' (for 'parody') 'thing-name' (for 'noun'), and 'many-wedder' (for 'bigamist').

Barnes's philological arguments are flawed by comic strangeness: in his wish to keep language accurately local, he made it arcane. Tellingly, the London-based Philological Society never asked him to become a member. As Chedzoy says: 'The great work of the Society was the preparation of its dictionary, which was eventually published as the *Oxford English Dictionary* in 1888, two years after Barnes's death. In their prospectus, the editors of the dictionary declared the principle that there should be no exclusions on the grounds of "obsoleteness, foreignness or localism", yet they almost completely ignored hundreds of revived items or neologisms suggested by Barnes in his various publications'.

In the face of such evidence, it's obvious that if we want to appreciate the power and purpose of Barnes's dialect poems, we have to accept their element of inventedness. Barnes claimed that he was producing something pure, simple, and old as the hills. ('I cannot help' writing in dialect, he once said; 'it is my mother tongue, and is to my mind the only true speech of the life that I draw.') In fact his work is immensely intricate, some-times a little crazy, and new. It is more like Burns than Clare, and more like Hugh MacDiarmid than either – a manner of speaking which is at once quaint (and therefore socially tolera-ble, however strange), and subversive (and therefore marginal).

Barnes's first dialect poems, written in 1834, were a series of eclogues modelled to varying degrees on Virgil's originals. They have been described and generally accepted as 'a half-humorous set of observations [of country working] people', which Barnes himself bracketed with all his other poems as merely 'pictures . . . I see in my mind'. Actually they are much more ambitious than that. Before writing the eclogues, he had dealt with conventional themes in standard English. Now he created a language which allowed him to deal directly with urgent contemporary problems.

The issue which forced Barnes to this creative crisis was enclosure – the subject of his first eclogue 'Rusticus Dolens, or Inclosures of Common', which was later re-titled 'Eclogue: The Common a-Took in'. The year he wrote this poem (1834), Dorset had been agitated by the Swing Riots, a series of distur-bances during which farm-workers protested about low wages, the price of bread, Irish labour, and the loss of traditional com-mon land. (The rioters rode through Hampshire, Wiltshire and Dorset, urging labourers to burn ricks and smash machines.) Barnes sympathized with the rioters, but being a cautious man, and preferring to avoid confrontation with authority, his response was not to show outright support. Instead, he offered a dramatic presentation of their cause – in poems like 'Father Come Hwome' and 'The 'Lotments'; as well as 'Eclogue: The Common a-Took in' itself. In this earliest example, two labour-ers, John and Thomas, discuss the effect of enclosures. John explains that he has to sell his geese because 'they do mean to take the moor in', and adds that he expects to have to sell the cow for the same reasons. Barnes suggests that once the two men lose their traditional rights, they will also forfeit their independence and their sense of belonging:

'Tis handy to live near a common;
But I've a zeed, an' I've a zaid,
That if a poor man got a bit o' bread,
They'll try to teake it vrom en.

'Eclogue: The Common a-Took in' ends with Thomas saying that 'I wer twold back t' other day,/ That they be got into a way/ O lettèn bits o' groun' out to the poor.' This hint of compromise no doubt derives in part from Barnes's reluctance to offend either the editor of the conservative *Dorset County Chronicle*, on which he depended for supplements to his income, or the parents of his pupils, who were his mainstay. Most of it, though, stems from his enduring respect for the status quo – a respect which underlay all his political and educational beliefs. (He was silent, for instance, about the conviction of the Tolpuddle Martyrs in 1834, having supported their claim for a living wage but opposed their means of achieving it.) He disapproved of organized labour (his poem 'The Times' depicts a typical Chartist as a cunning crow who deprives the labourer, a pig, of his roots). He extolled the virtues of the independent smallholder – 'my uncle Charles Rabbetts when he was free of debt and danger' – working in a feudal system. In *Views of Labour and Gold* (1859), his idiosyncratic textbook on economics, he states 'the squire and his lady are a great social good when they live among the poor, and keep before their eye the graceful pattern of Christian life, and raise the tone of feeling by kindness and sober expectation'.

In other words, Barnes's ideal society is a mixture of paternalistic conservatism and Christian socialism, combining elements from the writings of Ruskin, Morris, Kingsley and Samuel Smiles. But whereas his thinking often seems naive when he is writing prose or standard English, it becomes much subtler and more allusive when he turns to dialect. His poem 'Aïr an' Light' is a good case in point. Its third verse, in the 'national English' version, runs as follows:

The morning sun may cast abroad
    His light on dew about our feet,

And down below his noontide road
    The streams may glare below his heat;
The evening light may sparkle bright
    Across the quiv'ring gossamer;
But I, though fair he still may glow,
    Must miss a face he cannot show.

Compare this to the more energetic and evocative dialect version:

The mornèn zun do cast abroad
His light on drops o' dewy wet,
An' down below his noontide road
The streams do gleäre below his het;
His evenèn light do sparkle bright
Across the quiv'rèn gossamer;
But I, though fair he still mid glow,
Do miss a zight he cannot show.

The great majority of Barnes's dialect poems have a similar power: they may lack what Larkin called Hardy's 'bitter and ironical despair', but they prove that dialect widened his eyes and turned him into a poet who 'noticed things'. His Dorset is not a flimsy Arcadian paradise but a real place full of real people doing real work, and feeling real anxiety about change. In this respect, his work looks back to the Romantics, and forward to Edward Thomas, whose own poems often use definite characters and hard characteristics to create a landscape which is at once intimate and removed (in 'Lob', 'The Gypsy' and 'The Manor Farm', for instance). 'A Haulen o' the Corn' is a good example, with its attention to the sheer hard work of harvesting. So is 'Shroden Feäir', with its celebration of seasonal rituals, and 'Leady-Day, an' Ridden House', with its attention to domestic practicalities. These poems combine people and places and customs to create the picture of a community which has been superseded, but is still secure in the imaginative present. 'The Wold Wagon' is yet another example. Its technical terms and details make the poem part evocation and part elegy:

Upon his head an' tail wer pinks,
A-painted all in tangled links;
His two long zides wer blue, – his bed
Bent slightly upwards at the head;
His reaves rose upward in a bow
Above the slow hind-wheels below.

The imaginative pressure of these poems depends on more than a general feeling of dispossession: it is accelerated and deepened by three personal losses. One was the death of his son Julius, whom Barnes commemorated in 'To a Child Lost', 'Our Little Boy' and 'The Turnstile'. Another was the death of one of his brothers from sunstroke, which he remembered in 'The Child an' the Mowers', when writing about another boy in the neighbourhood who suffered the same fate. The lines derive a great deal of their power from remaining practical and pragmatic; they remind us that in the actual lives of labourers, shade is welcome and necessary:

Then they laid en there-right on the ground
    On a grass-heap, a-zweltrèn wi' het,
Wi' his heäir all a-wetted around
    His young feäce, wi' the big drops o' zweat;
In his little left palm he'd a-zet,
    Wi' his right hand, his vore-vinger's tip,
As ver zome'hat he woulden vorget,–
    Aye! zome thought that he woulden let slip.

The death of Barnes's wife Julia had an even more pervasive effect. He produced several elegies for her, in dialect and standard English, and they stand at the centre of his work in much the same way that 'Poems of 1912–13' do in Hardy's – but with no guilt stirred into their melancholy. In the earlier poems, written during their courtship, Barnes often told the story of his feelings by means of images to do with water. Water is cold and sometimes frozen in 'Orra', his narrative of frustration; in 'To

Julia' it is unlocked as 'the bright waves of the Frome'; in 'The Aquatic Excursion' it is 'glittering . . . up the stream' – and so on. This imagery returns in the best of his later poems about his wife, 'The Bwoat', where water carries the couple apart rather than uniting them:

Then, lik' a cloud below the skies,
A-drifted off, wi' less'nèn size
An' lost, she floated vrom my eyes,
    Where down below the stream did wind;
An' left the quiet weäves woonce mwore
To zink to rest, a sky-blue'd vloor,
Wi' all so still's the clote they bore,
    Aye, all but my own ruffled mind.

Barnes bends towards details under the weight of his bereavements: they are his consolation in a world stricken by bad luck, limited opportunities, and mortality. But he never loses his sense of larger consolations. When his reasons for despair are strongest, and his feelings of alienation most acute, he is still able to appeal to something outside himself for comfort – God, or Nature, or cyclical time. 'Time alone shall lead me on/ At last to where my love is gone', he writes in another poem for 'My Dearest Wife'. This leaves his work, like his life, rich in contradictions. His poems speak of a particular historical moment, yet his methods make him a voice apart. It was a combination Barnes often claimed not to notice in himself; in fact he knew it from first to last. When he had finished dictating his final poem, 'The Geäte A-Vallèn to', he turned to his daughter and said:

'Observe that word gate . . . that is how King Alfred would have pronounced it, and how it was called in the Saxon Chronicle, which told us of King Edward, who was slain at Corfe's gate.' He paused again, and continued: 'Ah! If the Court had not been moved to London, then the speech of King Alfred, of which our Dorset is the remnant, would have been the Court language of today'.

ANDREW MOTION

Note on the Text and Punctuation

For my selection of dialect poetry written by William Barnes and published during his lifetime, I have used his *Poems of Rural Life in the Dorset Dialect*, 1879 – which incorporates his dialect volumes published in 1844, 1859 and 1862, and was the last text he revised himself. In this copy-text I have silently corrected a number of small typographical errors.

For the text of dialect poems not published by Barnes during his lifetime, I have used manuscripts in the Dorset County Museum. My selection of Barnes's poems written in standard English is drawn from his *Poems Partly of Rural Life in National English*, 1846 and *Poems of Rural Life in Common English*, 1868 – and incorporates his subsequent revisions of these volumes – and also from a handful of other sources.

Throughout the dialect poems, I have restored the grave accents that are omitted in all recent editions of Barnes's poems; readers will find these accents helpful as pointers to rhythm and pronunciation.

Some Notes on Dorset Word-shapes

1. In *Poems of Rural Life in the Dorset Dialect*, 1879 Barnes gave 'a few hints on Dorset word-shapes'. The main sounds are:

i	*ee* in beet	v	*a* in father
ii	*e* in Dorset (a sound between (i) and (iii))	vi	*aw* in awe
		vii	*o* in dote
iii	*a* in mate	viii	*oo* in rood
iv	*i* in birth		

2. Dorset speech often has two sounds where standard English has one. Barnes used diaereses in his poems to indicate this. Other commonly used Dorset sounds are:

Dorset	d	Standard	th
	-ing		-en
	v		f
	z		s

3. Some words of unlike meanings which are sounded alike in standard English are not sounded alike in Dorset. For instance:

Dorset	twold (vii above)	Standard	told
	toll'd		toll'd
	meäre (i & iii)		mare
	mayor (v & i)		mayor
	païl (v & i)		pail
	peäle (i & iii)		pale

4. Dorset speech distinguishes between two classes of things:
a) personal things (e.g. man), for which the personal pronoun is 'he' and the demonstrative pronoun 'this' or 'that';
b) impersonal things (e.g. water), for which the personal pronoun is 'it', and the demonstrative pronoun 'this' or 'that'.

The objective case of 'he' is 'en', and of 'them', 'em'.

5. In Dorset speech, perfect participles often affix 'a–'.

6. In Dorset speech there are forms of strong and weak verbs which do not – or do not any longer – appear in standard English, for instance:

Dorset	scrope	Standard	scraped
	clomb		climbed

WILLIAM BARNES

The Blackbird

Ov all the birds upon the wing
Between the zunny show'rs o' spring,–
Vor all the lark, a-swingèn high,
Mid zing below a cloudless sky,
An' sparrows, clust'rèn roun' the bough,
Mid chatter to the men at plough,–
The blackbird, whisslèn in among
The boughs, do zing the gaÿest zong.

Vor we do hear the blackbird zing
His sweetest ditties in the spring,
When nippèn win's noo mwore do blow
Vrom northern skies, wi' sleet or snow,
But drēve light doust along between
The leäne-zide hedges, thick an' green;
An' zoo the blackbird in among
The boughs do zing the gaÿest zong.

'Tis blithe, wi' newly-open'd eyes,
To zee the mornèn's ruddy skies;
Or, out a-haulèn frith or lops
Vrom new-plēsh'd hedge or new vell'd copse,
To rest at noon in primrwose beds
Below the white-bark'd woak trees' heads;
But there's noo time, the whole daÿ long,
Lik' evenèn wi' the blackbird's zong.

Vor when my work is all a-done
Avore the zettèn o' the zun,
Then blushèn Jeäne do walk along
The hedge to meet me in the drong,

An' staÿ till all is dim an' dark
Bezides the ashen tree's white bark;
An' all bezides the blackbird's shrill
An 'runnèn evenèn-whissle's still.

An' there in bwoyhood I did rove
Wi' pryèn eyes along the drove
To vind the nest the blackbird meäde
O' grass-stalks in the high bough's sheäde:
Or clim' aloft, wi' clingèn knees,
Vor crows' aggs up in swaÿèn trees,
While frighten'd blackbirds down below
Did chatter o' their little foe.
An' zoo there's noo pleäce lik' the drong,
Where I do hear the blackbird's zong.

drēve, *drive*; frith, *brushwood*; lops, *kindling sticks*; plēsh, *to lay a hedge by
pegging down the cut stems*; drong, *a narrow way*

Vellèn o' the Tree

Aye, the girt elem tree out in little hwome groun'
Wer a-stannèn this mornèn, an' now's a-cut down.
Aye, the girt elem tree, so big roun' an' so high,
Where the mowers did goo to their drink, an' did lie
In the sheäde ov his head, when the zun at his heighth
Had a-drove em vrom mowèn, wi' het an' wi' drith,
Where the haÿ-meäkers put all their picks an' their reäkes,
An' did squot down to snabble their cheese an' their ceäkes,
An' did vill vrom their flaggons their cups wi' their eäle,
An' did meäke theirzelves merry wi' joke an wi' teäle.

Ees, we took up a rwope an' we tied en all round
At the top o'n, wi' woone end a-hangèn to ground,
An' we cut, near the ground, his girt stem a'most drough,
An' we bent the wold head o'n wi' woone tug or two;
An' he swaÿ'd all his limbs, an' he nodded his head,
Till he vell away down like a pillar o' lead:
An' as we did run vrom en, there, clwose at our backs,
Oh! his boughs come to groun' wi' sich whizzes an' cracks;
An' his top wer so lofty that, now he is down,
The stem o'n do reach a'most over the groun'.
Zoo the girt elem tree out in little hwome groun',
Wer a-stannèn this mornèn, an' now's a-cut down.

girt, *great*; drith, *dryness, thirst*; het, *heat*; squot, *squat (also to flatten at a blow)*; snabble, *snap up quickly*

5

Eclogue: The 'Lotments
John and Richard

JOHN

Zoo you be in your groun' then, I do zee,
A-workèn and a-zingèn lik' a bee.
How do it answer? what d'ye think about it?
D'ye think 'tis better wi' it than without it?
A-reck'nèn rent, an' time, an' zeed to stock it,
D'ye think that you be any thing in pocket?

RICHARD

O, 'tis a goodish help to woone, I'm sure o't.
If I had not a-got it, my poor bwones
Would now ha' eäch'd a-crackèn stwones
Upon the road; I wish I had zome mwore o't.

JOHN

I wish the girt woones had a-got the greäce
To let out land lik this in ouer pleäce;
But I do fear there'll never be nwone vor us,
An I can't tell whatever we shall do:
We be a most a-starvèn, an' we'd goo
To 'merica, if we'd enough to car us.

RICHARD

Why 'twer the squire, good now! a worthy man,
That vu'st brought into ouer pleäce the plan;
He zaid he'd let a vew odd eäcres
O' land to us poor leäb'rèn men;
An', faïth, he had enough o' teäkers
Vor that, an' twice so much ageän.
Zoo I took zome here, near my hovel,
To exercise my speäde an' shovel;
An' what wi' dungèn, diggèn up, an' zeedèn,
A-thinnèn, cleänèn, howèn up an' weedèn,

I, an' the biggest o' the children too,
Do always vind some useful jobs to do.

JOHN

Aye, wi' a bit o' ground, if woone got any,
Woone's bwoys can soon get out an' eärn a penny;
An' then, by workèn, they do learn the vaster
The way to do things when they have a meäster;
Vor woone must know a deäl about the land
Bevore woone's fit to lend a useful hand,
In geärden or a-vield upon a farm.

RICHARD

An' then the work do keep em out o' harm;
Vor vo'ks that don't do nothèn wull be vound
Soon doèn woorse than nothèn, I'll be bound.
But as vor me, d'ye zee, wi' theäse here bit
O' land, why I have ev'ry thing a'mwost:
Vor I can fatten vowels vor the spit,
Or zell a good fat goose or two to rwoast;
An' have my beäns or cabbage, greens or grass,
Or bit o' wheat, or, sich my happy feäte is,
That I can keep a little cow, or ass,
An' a vew pigs to eat the little teäties.

JOHN

An' when your pig's a-fatted pretty well
Wi' teäties, or wi' barley an' some bran,
Why you've a-got zome vlitches vor to zell,
Or hang in chimney-corner, if you can.

RICHARD

Aye, that's the thing; an' when the pig do die,
We got a lot ov offal vor to fry,
An' netlèns vor to bwoil; or put the blood in,
An' meäke a meal or two o'good black-pudden.

JOHN

I'd keep myzelf from parish, I'd be bound,
If I could get a little patch o' ground.

netlèns, *a food of pig's innards*

Uncle an' Aunt

How happy uncle us'd to be
O' zummer time, when aunt an' he
O' Zunday evenèns, eärm in eärm,
Did walk about their tiny farm,
While birds did zing an' gnats did zwarm,
Drough grass a'most above their knees,
An' roun' by hedges an' by trees
   Wi' leafy boughs a-swaÿen.

His hat wer broad, his cwoat wer brown,
Wi' two long flaps a-hangèn down;
An' vrom his knee went down a blue
Knit stockèn to his buckled shoe;
An' aunt did pull her gown-taïl drough
Her pocket-hole, to keep en neat,
As she mid walk, or teäke a seat
   By leafy boughs a-swaÿèn.

An' vu'st they'd goo to zee their lots
O' pot-eärbs in the geärden plots;
An' he, i'-may-be, by the hatch,
Would zee aunt's vowls upon a patch
O'zeeds, an' vow if he could catch
Em wi' his gun, they shoudden vlee
Noo mwore into their roostèn tree
   Wi' leafy boughs a-swaÿèn.

An' then vrom geärden they did pass
Drough orcha'd out to zee the grass,
An' if the apple-blooth, so white,
Mid be at all a-touch'd wi' blight;
An' uncle, happy at the zight,

Did guess what cider there mid be
In all the orcha'd, tree wi' tree
    Wi' tutties all a-swaÿen.

An' then they stump'd along vrom there
A-vield, to zee the cows an' meäre;
An' she, when uncle come in zight,
Look'd up, an' prick'd her ears upright,
An' whicker'd out wi' all her might;
An' he, a-chucklèn, went to zee
The cows below the sheädy tree
    Wi' leafy boughs a-swaÿen.

An' last ov all, they went to know
How vast the grass in meäd did grow;
An' then aunt zaid 'twer time to goo
In hwome, – a-holdèn up her shoe,
To show how wet he wer wi' dew.
An' zoo they toddled hwome to rest,
Lik' doves a-vleèn to their nest
    In leafy boughs a-swaÿen.

blooth, *blossom in the mass*; tutties, *nosegays*; whicker'd, *neighed*

Hay-Meäkèn

'Tis merry ov a zummer's day,
Where vo'k be out a-meäkèn haÿ;
Where men an'women, in a string,
Do ted or turn the grass, an' zing,
Wi' cheemèn vaïces, merry zongs,
A-tossèn o' their sheenèn prongs
Wi' eärms a-zwangèn left an' right,
In colour'd gowns an' shirtsleeves white;
Or, wider spread, a-reäkèn round
The rwosy hedges o' the ground,
Where Sam do zee the speckled sneäke,
An' try to kill en wi' his reäke;
An Poll do jump about an' squall,
To zee the twistèn slooworm crawl.

'Tis merry where a gaÿ-tongued lot
Ov haÿ-meäkers be all a-squot,
On lightly-russlèn haÿ, a-spread
Below an elem's lofty head,
To rest their weary limbs an' munch
Their bit o' dinner, or their nunch;
Where teethy reäkes do lie all round
By picks a-stuck up into ground.
An' wi' their vittles in their laps,
An' in their hornen cups their draps
O' cider sweet, or frothy eäle,
Their tongues do run wi' joke an' teäle.

An' when the zun, so low an' red,
Do sheen above the leafy head
O' zome broad tree, a-rizèn high
Avore the vi'ry western sky,
'Tis merry where all han's do goo
Athirt the groun', by two an' two,

11

A-reäkèn, over humps an' hollors,
The russlèn grass up into rollers.
An' woone do row it into line,
An' woone do clwose it up behine;
An' after them the little bwoys
Do stride an' fling their eärms all woys,
Wi' busy picks, an' proud young looks
A-meäkèn up their tiny pooks.
An' zoo 'tis merry out among
The vo'k in haÿ-vield all day long.

ted, *throw hay aboard to dry*; nunch, *a bit of food*; pook, *stook of hay*

The Clote
(Water-Lily)

O zummer clote! when the brook's a-glidèn
   So slow an' smooth down his zedgy bed,
Upon thy broad leaves so seäfe a-ridèn
    The water's top wi' thy yollow head,
      By alder's heads, O,
      An' bulrush beds, O,
Thou then dost float, goolden zummer clote!

The grey-bough'd withy's a-leänèn lowly
   Above the water thy leaves do hide;
The bendèn bulrush, a-swaÿèn slowly,
    Do skirt in zummer thy river's zide;
      An' perch in shoals, O,
      Do vill the holes, O,
Where thou dost float, goolden zummer clote!

Oh! when thy brook-drinkèn flow'r 's a-blowèn,
   The burnèn zummer's a-zettèn in;
The time o'greenness, the time o'mowèn,
    When in the haÿ-vield, wi' zunburnt skin,
      The vo'k do drink, O,
      Upon the brink, O,
Where thou dost float, goolden zummer clote!

Wi' eärms a-spreadèn, an' cheäks a-blowèn,
   How proud wer I when I vu'st could zwim
Athirt the pleäce where thou bist a-growèn,
    Wi' thy long more vrom the bottom dim;
      While cows, knee-high, O,
      In brook, wer nigh, O,
Where thou dost float, goolden zummer clote!

Ov all the brooks drough the meäds a-windèn,
   Ov all the meäds by a river's brim,

There's nwone so feäir o' my own heart's vindèn,
   As where the maïdens do zee thee zwim,
      An' stan' to teäke, O,
      Wi' long-stemm'd reäke, O,
Thy flow'r afloat, goolden zummer clote!

athirt, *athwart*; more, *mooring rope (i.e., root)*

Shrodon Feäir
The vu'st peärt

An' zoo's the day wer warm an' bright,
An' nar a cloud wer up in zight,
We wheedled father vor the meäre
An' cart, to goo to Shrodon feäir.
An' Poll an' Nan run off up stairs,
To shift their things, as wild as heäres;
An' pull'd out, each o'm vrom her box,
Their snow-white leäce an' newest frocks,
An' put their bonnets on, a-lined
Wi' blue, an' sashes tied behind;
An' turn'd avore the glass their feäce
An' back, to zee their things in pleäce;
While Dick an' I did brush our hats
An' cwoats, an' cleän ourzelves lik' cats.
At woone or two o'clock, we vound
Ourzelves at Shrodon seäfe and sound,
A-struttèn in among the rows
O' tilted stannèns an' o' shows,
An' girt long booths wi' little bars
Chock-vull o' barrels, mugs, an' jars,
An' meat a-cookèn out avore
The vier at the upper door;
Where zellers bwold to buyers shy
Did hollow round us, 'What d'ye buy?'
An' scores o' merry tongues did speak
At woonce, an children's pipes did squeak,
An' horns did blow, an' drums did rumble,
An' bawlèn merrymen did tumble;
An' woone did all but want an edge
To peärt the crowd wi', lik' a wedge.

We zaw the dancers in a show
Dance up an' down, an' to an' fro,
Upon a rwope, wi' chalky zoles,
So light as magpies up on poles;
An' tumblers, wi' their streaks an' spots,
That all but tied theirzelves in knots.
An' then a conjurer burn'd off
Poll's han'kerchief so black's a snoff,
An' het en, wi' a single blow,
Right back ageän so white as snow.
An' after that, he fried a fat
Girt ceäke inzide o' my new hat;
An' yet, vor all he did en brown,
He didden even zweal the crown.

stannèns, *fair or market stalls*; snoff, *candle snuffer*; zweal, *scorch*

Shrodon Feäir
The rest o't

An' after that we met wi' zome
O' Mans'on vo'k, but jist a-come,
An' had a raffle vor a treat
All roun', o' gingerbread to eat;
An' Tom meäde leäst, wi' all his sheäkes,
An' païd the money vor the ceäkes,
But wer so lwoth to put it down
As if a penny wer a poun'.
Then up come zidelèn Sammy Heäre,
That's fond o' Poll, an' she can't bear,
A-holdèn out his girt scram vist,
An' ax'd her, wi' a grin an' twist,
To have zome nuts; an' she, to hide
Her laughèn, turn'd her head azide,
An' answer'd that she'd rather not,
But Nancy mid. An' Nan, so hot
As vier, zaid 'twer quite enough
Vor Poll to answer vor herzuf:
She had a tongue, she zaid, an' wit
Enough to use en, when 'twer fit.
An' in the dusk, a-ridèn round
Drough Okford, who d'ye think we vound
But Sam ageän, a-gwaïn vrom feäir
Astride his broken-winded meäre.
An' zoo, a-hettèn her, he tried
To keep up clwose by ouer zide:
But when we come to Haÿward-brudge,
Our Poll gi'ed Dick a meänèn nudge,
An' wi' a little twitch our meäre
Flung out her lags so light's a heäre,
An' left poor Sammy's skin an' bwones
Behind, a-kickèn o' the stwones.

Eclogue: The Common a-Took in
Thomas an' John

THOMAS

Good morn t'ye, John. How b'ye? how b'ye?
Zoo you be gwaïn to market, I do zee.
Why, you be quite a-lwoaded wi' your geese.

JOHN

Ees, Thomas, ees.
Why, I'm a-gettèn rid ov ev'ry goose
An' goslèn I've a-got: an' what is woose,
I fear that I must zell my little cow.

THOMAS

How zoo, then, John? Why, what's the matter now?
What, can't ye get along? B'ye run a-ground?
An' can't paÿ twenty shillèns vor a pound?
What, can't ye put a lwoaf on shelf?

JOHN

Ees, now;
But I do fear I shan't 'ithout my cow.
No; they do meän to teäke the moor in, I do hear,
An' 'twill be soon begun upon;
Zoo I must zell my bit o' stock to-year,
Because they woon't have any groun' to run upon.

THOMAS

Why, what d'ye tell o'? I be very zorry
To hear what they be gwaïn about;
But yet I s'pose there'll be a 'lotment vor ye,
When they do come to mark it out.

JOHN

No; not vor me, I fear. An' if there should,
Why 'twoulden be so handy as 'tis now;

18

Vor 'tis the common that do do me good,
The run vor my vew geese, or vor my cow.

THOMAS

Ees, that's the job; why 'tis a handy thing
To have a bit o' common, I do know,
To put a little cow upon in Spring,
The while woone's bit ov orcha'd grass do grow.

JOHN

Aye, that's the thing, you zee. Now I do mow
My bit o' grass, an' meäke a little rick;
An' in the zummer, while do grow,
My cow do run in common vor to pick
A bleäde or two o' grass, if she can vind em,
Vor tother cattle don't leäve much behind em.
Zoo in the evenèn, we do put a lock
O' nice fresh grass avore the wicket;
An' she do come at vive or zix o'clock,
As constant as the zun, to pick it.
An' then, bezides the cow, why we do let
Our geese run out among the emmet hills;
An' then when we do pluck em, we do get
Vor zeäle zome veathers an' zome quills;
An' in the winter we do fat em well,
An' car em to the market vor to zell
To gentlevo'ks, vor we don't oft avvword
To put a goose a-top ov ouer bwoard;
But we do get our feäst, – vor we be eäble
To clap the giblets up a-top o' teäble.

THOMAS

An' I don't know o' many better things,
Than geese's heads and gizzards, lags an' wings.

JOHN

An' then, when I ha' nothèn else to do,
Why I can teäke my hook an' gloves, an' goo

To cut a lot o' vuzz and briars
Vor hetèn ovens, or vor lightèn viers.
An' when the children be too young to eärn
A penny, they can g'out in zunny weather,
An' run about, an' get together
A bag o' cow-dung vor to burn.

THOMAS
'Tis handy to live near a common;
But I've a-zeed, an' I've a-zaid,
That if a poor man got a bit o' bread,
They'll try to teäke it vrom en.
But I wer twold back tother day,
That they be got into a way
O' lettèn bits o' groun' out to the poor.

JOHN
Well, I do hope 'tis true, I'm sure;
An' I do hope that they will do it here,
Or I must goo to workhouse, I do fear.

wicket, *door*; emmet hills, *anthills*; vuzz, *furze, gorse*

The Happy Days When I wer Young

In happy days when I wer young,
An' had noo ho, an' laugh'd an' zung,
The maïd wer merry by her cow,
An' men wer merry wi' the plough;
But never talk'd, at hwome or out
O' doors, o' what's a-talk'd about
By many now, – that to despise
The laws o' God an' man is wise.
Wi' daïly health, an' daïly bread,
An' thatch above their shelter'd head,
They velt noo fear, an' had noo spite,
To keep their eyes awake at night;
But slept in peace wi' God on high
An' man below, an' fit to die.

O grassy meäd an' woody nook,
An' waters o' the windèn brook,
That sprung below the vu'st dark sky
That raïn'd, to run till seas be dry;
An' hills a-stannèn on while all
The works o' man do rise an' vall;
An' trees the toddlèn child do vind
At vu'st, an' leäve at last behind;
I wish that you could now unvwold
The peace an' jaÿ o' times o' wold;
An' tell, when death do still my tongue,
O' happy days when I wer young.
Vrom where wer all this venom brought,
To kill our hope an' taïnt our thought?
Clear brook! thy water coulden bring
Such venom vrom thy rocky spring;

Nor could it come in zummer blights,
Or reävèn storms o' winter nights,
Or in the cloud an' viry stroke
O' thunder that do split the woak.

O valley dear! I wish that I
'D a-liv'd in former times, to die
Wi' all the happy souls that trod
Thy turf in peäce, an' died to God;
Or gone wi' them that laugh'd an' zung
In happy days when I wer young!

ho, *care*

The Carter

O, I be a carter, wi' my whip
   A-smackèn loud, as by my zide,
Up over hill, an' down the dip,
   The heavy lwoad do slowly ride.

An' I do haul in all the crops,
   An' I do bring in vuzz vrom down;
An' I do goo vor wood to copse,
   An' car the corn an' straw to town.

An' I do goo vor lime, an' bring
   Hwome cider wi' my sleek-heäir'd team,
An' smack my limber whip an' zing,
   While all their bells do gaïly cheeme.

An' I do always know the pleäce
   To gi'e the hosses breath, or drug;
An' ev'ry hoss do know my feäce,
   An' mind my *'mether ho!* an' *whug!*

An' merry haÿ-meäkers do ride
   Vrom vield in zummer wi' their prongs,
In my blue waggon, zide by zide
   Upon the reäves, a-zingèn zongs.

An' when the vrost do catch the stream,
   An' oves wi' icicles be hung,
My pantèn hosses' breath do steam
   In white-grass'd vields, a-haulèn dung.

An' mine's the waggon fit vor lwoads,
   An' mine be lwoads to cut a rout;
An' mine's a team, in routy rwoads,
   To pull a lwoaded waggon out.

A zull is nothèn when do come
   Behind their lags; an' they do teäke

A roller as they would a drum,
  An' harrow as they would a reäke.

O! I be a carter, wi' my whip
  A-smackèn loud, as by my zide,
Up over hill, an' down the dip,
  The heavy lwoad do slowly ride.

limber, *limp*; drug, *drag for a wheel*; 'mether ho, *come hither*; whug, *go off to the right*; oves, *eaves*; rout, *rut*; zull, *plough*

Eclogue: Father Come Hwome
John, Wife, an' Child

CHILD

O mother, mother! be the teäties done?
Here's father now a-comèn down the track.
He's got his nitch o' wood upon his back,
An' such a speäker in en! I'll be bound,
He's long enough to reach vrom ground
Up to the top ov ouer tun;
'Tis jist the very thing vor Jack an' I
To goo a-colepecksèn wi', by an' by.

WIFE

The teäties must be ready pretty nigh;
Do teäke woone up upon the fork an' try.
The ceäke upon the vier, too, 's a-burnèn,
I be afeärd: do run an' zee, an' turn en.

JOHN

Well, mother! here I be woonce mwore, at hwome.

WIFE

Ah! I be very glad you be a-come.
You be a-tired an' cwold enough, I s'pose;
Zit down an' rest your bwones, an' warm your nose.

JOHN

Why I be nippy: what is there to eat?

WIFE

Your supper's nearly ready. I've a-got
Some teäties here a-doèn in the pot;
I wish wi' all my heart I had some meat.
I got a little ceäke too, here, a-beäkèn o'n
Upon the vier. 'Tis done by this time though.

He's nice an' moist; vor when I wer a-meäkén o'n
I stuck some bits ov apple in the dough.

CHILD

Well, father; what d'ye think? The pig got out
This mornèn; an' avore we zeed or heärd en,
He run about, an' got out into geärden,
An' routed up the groun' zoo wi' his snout!

JOHN

Now only think o' that! You must contrive
To keep en in, or else he'll never thrive.

CHILD

An' father, what d'ye think? I voun' to-day
The nest where thik wold hen ov our's do lay:
'Twer out in orcha'd hedge, an' had vive aggs.

WIFE

Lo'k there: how wet you got your veet an' lags!
How did ye get in such a pickle, Jahn?

JOHN

I broke my hoss, an' been a-fwo'ced to stan'
All's day in mud an' water vor to dig,
An' meäde myzelf so wetshod as a pig.

CHILD

Father, teäke off your shoes, then come, and I
Will bring your wold woones vor ye, nice an' dry.

WIFE

An' have ye got much hedgen mwore to do?

JOHN

Enough to last vor dree weeks mwore or zoo.

WIFE

An' when y'ave done the job you be about,
D'ye think you'll have another vound ye out?

JOHN

O ees, there'll be some mwore: vor after that,
I got a job o' trenchèn to goo at;
An' then zome trees to shroud, an' wood to vell,–
Zoo I do hope to rub on pretty well
Till zummer time; an' then I be to cut
The wood an' do the trenchèn by the tut.

CHILD

An' nex' week, father, I'm a-gwaïn to goo
A-pickèn stwones, d'ye know, vor Farmer True.

WIFE

An' little Jack, you know, 's a-gwaïn to eärn
A penny too, a-keepèn birds off corn.

JOHN

O brave! What wages do 'e meän to gi'e?

WIFE

She dreppence vor a day, an' twopence he.

JOHN

Well, Polly; thou must work a little spracker
When thou bist out, or else thou wu'ten pick
A dungpot lwoad o' stwones up very quick.

CHILD

Oh! yes I shall. But Jack do want a clacker:
An' father, wull ye teäke an' cut
A stick or two to meäke his hut?

JOHN

You wench! why you be always up a-baggèn.
I be too tired now to-night, I'm sure,
    To zet a-doèn any mwore:
Zoo I shall goo up out o' the waÿ o' the waggon.

teäties, *potatoes*; nitch, *bundle of firewood*; speäker, *spiker, i.e., stick used to carry firewood over the shoulder*; colepecksèn, *cullpecking, i.e. beating down apples left on trees after main crop has been taken in*; nippy, *hungry*; hoss, *horse, or plank of wood on which ditchers stand when digging*; trees to shroud, *cut lower branches of trees*; by the tut, *by the job or piece, not by the day*; spracker, *livelier*; hut, *birdkeeper's house*; out o' the waÿ o' the waggon, *upstairs in bed*

The Hwomestead

If I had all the land my zight
   Can overlook vrom Chalwell hill,
Vrom Sherborn left to Blanvord right,
   Why I could be but happy still.
An' I be happy wi' my spot
O' freehold ground an' mossy cot,
An' shoulden get a better lot
   If I had all my will.

My orcha'd's wide, my trees be young;
   An' they do bear such heavy crops,
Their boughs, lik' onion-rwopes a-hung,
   Be all a-trigg'd to year, wi' props.
I got some geärden groun' to dig,
A parrock, an' a cow an' pig;
I got zome cider vor to swig,
   An' eäle o' malt an' hops.

I'm landlord o' my little farm,
   I'm king 'ithin my little pleäce;
I don't break laws, an' don't do harm,
   An' ben't a-feär'd o' noo man's feäce.
When I'm a-cover'd wi' my thatch,
Noo man do deäre to lift my latch;
Where honest han's do shut the hatch,
   There fear do leäve the pleäce.

My lofty elem trees do screen
   My brown-ruf'd house, an' here below,
My geese do strut athirt the green,
   An' hiss an' flap their wings o' snow;
As I do walk along a rank
Ov apple trees, or by a bank,
Or zit upon a bar or plank,
   To zee how things do grow.

Uncle out o' Debt an' out o' Danger

Ees; uncle had thik small hwomestead,
The leäzes an' the bits o' meäd,
Bezides the orcha'd in his prime,
An' copse-wood vor the winter time.
His wold black meäre, that draw'd his cart,
An' he, wer seldom long apeärt;
Vor he work'd hard an' païd his woy,
An' zung so litsome as a bwoy,
    As he toss'd an' work'd,
    An' blow'd an' quirk'd,
'I'm out o' debt an' out o' danger,
  An' I can feäce a friend or stranger;
I've a vist for friends, an' I'll vind a peäir
Vor the vu'st that do meddle wi' me or my meäre.'

His meäre's long vlexy vetlocks grow'd
Down roun' her hoofs so black an' brode;
Her head hung low, her taïl reach'd down
A-bobbèn nearly to the groun'.
The cwoat that uncle mwostly wore
Wer long behind an' straïght avore,
An' in his shoes he had girt buckles,
An' breeches button'd round his huckles;
    An' he zung wi' pride,
    By's wold meäre's zide,
'I'm out o' debt an' out o' danger,
  An' I can feäce a friend or stranger;
I've a vist vor friends, an' I'll vind a peäir
Vor the vu'st that do meddle wi' me or my meäre.'

An' he would work, – an' lwoad, an' shoot,
An' spur his heaps o' dung or zoot;
Or car out haÿ, to sar his vew
Milch cows in corners dry an' lew;

Or dreve a zyve, or work a pick,
To pitch or meäke his little rick;
Or thatch en up wi' straw or zedge,
Or stop a shard, or gap, in hedge;
    An' he work'd an' flung
    His eärms, an' zung
'I'm out o' debt an' out o' danger,
  An' I can feäce a friend or stranger;
I've a vist vor friends, an' I'll vind a peäir
Vor the vu'st that do meddle wi' me or my meäre.'

An' when his meäre an' he'd a-done
Their work, an' tired ev'ry bwone,
He zot avore the vire, to spend
His evenèn wi' his wife or friend;
An' wi' his lags out-stratch'd vor rest,
An' woone hand in his wes'coat breast,
While burnèn sticks did hiss an' crack,
An' fleämes did bleäzy up the back,
    There he zung so proud
    In a bakky cloud,
'I'm out o' debt an' out o' danger,
  An' I can feäce a friend or stranger;
I've a vist vor friends, an' I'll vind a peäir
Vor the vu'st that do meddle wi' me or my meäre.'

From market how he used to ride,
Wi' pots a-bumpèn by his zide
Wi' things a-bought – but not vor trust,
Vor what he had he païd vor vu'st;
An' when he trotted up the yard,
The calves did bleäry to be sar'd,
An' pigs did scoat all drough the muck,
An' geese did hiss, an' hens did cluck;
    An' he zung aloud,
    So pleased an' proud,

'I'm out o' debt an' out o' danger,
    An' I can feäce a friend or stranger;
I've a vist vor friends, an' I'll vind a peäir
Vor the vu'st that do meddle wi' me or my meäre.'

    When he wer joggèn hwome woone night
    Vrom market, after candle-light,
        (He mid a-took a drop o' beer,
        Or midden, vor he had noo fear,)
    Zome ugly, long-lagg'd, herrèn-ribs,
    Jump'd out an' ax'd en vor his dibs;
    But he soon gi'ed en such a mawlèn,
    That there he left en down a-sprawlèn,
        While he jogg'd along
        Wi' his own wold zong,
    'I'm out o' debt an' out o' danger,
        An' I can feäce a friend or stranger;
I've a vist vor friends, an' I'll vind a peäir
Vor the vu'st that do meddle wi' me or my meäre.'

litsome, *happy*; quirk'd, *grunt*; spur his heaps o' dung or zoot, *cast it
abroad*; sar, *serve, give food to cattle*; lew, *sheltered*; dreve a zyve, *use a
scythe*; shard, *small gap in a hedge*; bleary to be sar'd, *low to be fed*; scoat,
run away quickly; herrèn-ribs, *lanky person*; dibs, *coins*

The Wold Waggon

The girt wold waggon uncle had,
When I wer up a hardish lad,
Did stand, a-screen'd vrom het an' wet,
In zummer at the barken geäte,
Below the elems' spreädèn boughs,
A-rubb'd by all the pigs an' cows.
An' I've a-clom his head an' zides,
A-riggèn up or jumpèn down
A-plaÿèn, or in happy rides
Along the leäne or drough the groun'.
An' many souls be in their greäves,
That rod' together on his reäves;
An' he, an' all the hosses too,
'V a-ben a-done vor years agoo.

Upon his head an' tail wer pinks,
A-païnted all in tangled links;
His two long zides wer blue, – his bed
Bent slightly upward at the head;
His reäves rose upward in a bow
Above the slow hind-wheels below.
Vour hosses wer a-kept to pull
The girt wold waggon when 'twer vull:
The black meäre *Smiler*, strong enough
To pull a house down by herzuf,
So big, as took my widest strides
To straddle halfway down her zides;
An' champèn *Vi'let*, sprack an' light,
That foam'd an' pull'd wi' all her might:
An' *Whitevoot*, leäzy in the treäce,
Wi' cunnèn looks an' snow-white feäce;
Bezides a baÿ woone, short-taïl *Jack*,
That wer a treäce-hoss or a hack.

How many lwoads o' vuzz, to scald
The milk, thik waggon have a-haul'd!
An' wood vrom copse, an' poles vor raïls,
An' bavèns wi' their bushy taïls;
An' loose-ear'd barley, hangèn down
Outzide the wheels a'móst to groun',
An' lwoads o' haÿ so sweet an' dry,
A-builded straïght, an' long, an' high;
An' häy-meäkers a-zittèn roun'
The reäves, a-ridèn hwome vrom groun',
When Jim gi'ed Jenny's lips a-smackèn,
An' jealous Dicky whipp'd his back,
An' maïdens scream'd to veel the thumps
A-gi'ed by trenches an' by humps.
But he, an' all his hosses too,
'V a-ben a-done vor years agoo.

barken, *cow-yard*; reäves, *frame on wagon side that keeps the load above the wheels*; treäce, *trace*; bavèns, *faggots of brushwood*

The Common a-Took in

Oh! no, Poll, no! Since they've a-took
The common in, our lew wold nook
Don't seem a-bit as used to look
   When we had runnèn room;
Girt banks do shut up ev'ry drong,
An' stratch wi' thorny backs along
Where we did use to run among
   The vuzzen an' the broom.

Ees; while the ragged colts did crop
The nibbled grass, I used to hop
The emmet-buts, vrom top to top,
   So proud o'my spry jumps:
Wi' thee behind or at my zide,
A-skippèn on so light an' wide
'S thy little frock would let thee stride,
   Among the vuzzy humps.

Ah while the lark up over head
Did twitter, I did search the red
Thick bunch o' broom, or yollow bed
   O' vuzzen vor a nest;
An' thou di'st hunt about, to meet
Wi' strawberries so red an' sweet,
Or clogs, or shoes off hosses' veet,
   Or wild thyme vor thy breast;

Or when the cows did run about
A-stung, in zummer, by the stout,
Or when they playd, or when they foüght,
   Di'st stand a-lookèn on:
An' where white geese, wi' long red bills,
Did veed among the emmet-hills,
There we did goo to vind their quills
   Alongzide o' the pon'.

What fun there wer among us, when
The haÿward come, wi' all his men,
To drève the common, an' to pen
    Strange cattle in the pound;
The cows did bleäre, the men did shout
An' toss their eärms an' sticks about,
An' vo'ks, to own their stock, come out
    Vrom all the housen round.

stout, *cowfly or gadfly*; haÿward, *warden of a common*; drève, *drive, herd all the animals on the common*

The Music o' the Dead

When music, in a heart that's true,
Do kindle up wold loves anew,
An' dim wet eyes, in feäirest lights,
Do zee but inward fancy's zights;
When creepèn years, wi' with'rèn blights,
  'V a-took off them that wer so dear,
  How touchèn 'tis if we do hear
    The tuèns o' the dead, John.

When I, a-stannèn in the lew
O' trees a storm's a-beätèn drough,
Do zee the slantèn mist a-drove
By spitevul winds along the grove,
An' hear their hollow sounds above
  My shelter'd head, do seem, as I
  Do think o' zunny days gone by,
    Lik' music vor the dead, John.

Last night, as I wer gwaïn along
The brook, I heärd the milk-maïd's zong
A-ringèn out so clear an' shrill
Along the meäds an' roun' the hill.
I catch'd the tuèn, an' stood still
  To hear't; 'twer woone that Jeäne did zing
  A-vield a-milkèn in the spring,—
    Sweet music o' the dead, John.

Don't tell o' zongs that be a-zung
By young chaps now, wi' sheämeless tongue:
Zing me wold ditties, that would start
The maïdens' tears, or stir my heart
To teäke in life a manly peärt,—

The wold vo'k's zongs that twold a teäle,
An' vollow'd round their mugs o' eäle,
    The music o' the dead, John.

lew, *shelter*

The Hwomestead a-Vell into Hand

The house where I wer born an' bred,
  Did own his woaken door, John,
When vu'st he shelter'd father's head,
  An' gramfer's long avore, John.
An' many a ramblèn happy chile,
  An' chap so strong an' bwold,
An' bloomèn maïd wi' playsome smile,
  Did call their hwome o' wold
    Thik ruf so warm,
    A-kept vrom harm
By elem trees that broke the storm.

An' in the orcha'd out behind,
  The apple-trees in row, John,
Did sway wi' moss about their rind
  Their heads a-noddèn low, John.
An' there, bezide zome groun' vor corn,
  Two strips did skirt the road;
In woone the cow did toss her horn,
  While tother wer a-mow'd,
    In June, below
    The lofty row
Ov trees that in the hedge did grow.

A-workèn in our little patch
    O' parrock, rathe or leäte, John,
We little ho'd how vur mid stratch
    The squier's wide esteäte, John.
Our hearts, so honest an' so true,
    Had little vor to fear;
Vor we could paÿ up all their due,
    An' gi'e a friend good cheer
        At hwome, below
        The lofty row
O' trees a-swaÿèn to an' fro.

An' there in het, an' there in wet,
    We tweil'd wi' busy hands, John;
Vor ev'ry stroke o' work we het,
    Did better our own lands, John.
But after me, ov all my kin,
    Not woone can hold em on;
Vor we can't get a life put in
    Vor mine, when I'm a-gone
        Vrom thik wold brown
        Thatch ruf, a-boun'
By elem trees a-growèn roun'.

Ov eight good hwomes, where I can mind
    Vo'k liv'd upon their land, John,
But dree be now a-left behind;
    The rest ha' vell in hand, John,
An' all the happy souls they ved
    Be scatter'd vur an' wide.
An' zome o'm be a-wantèn bread,
    Zome, better off, ha' died,
        Noo mwore to ho
        Vor homes below
The trees a-swaÿèn to an' fro.

An' I could leäd ye now all round
   The parish, if I would, John,
An' show ye still the very ground
   Where vive good housen stood, John.
In broken orcha'ds near the spot,
   A vew wold trees do stand;
But dew do vall where vo'k woonce zot
   About the burnèn brand
      In housen warm,
         A-kept vrom harm
By elems that did break the storm.

gramfer, *grandfather*; rind, *bark*; strips, *narrow fields*; ho'd, *cared*; tweil'd,
worked

Eclogue: The Times
John an' Tom

JOHN

Well, Tom, how be'st? Zoo thou'st a-got thy neäme
Among the leaguers, then, as I've a-heärd.

TOM

Aye, John, I have, John; an' I ben't afeärd
To own it. Why, who woulden do the seäme?
We shan't goo on lik' this long, I can tell ye.
Bread is so high an' wages be so low,
That, after workèn lik' a hoss, you know,
A man can't eärn enough to vill his belly.

JOHN

Ah! well! Now there, d'ye know, if I wer sure
That theäsem men would gi'e me work to do
All drough the year, an' always paÿ me mwore
Than I'm a-eärnèn now, I'd jein em too.
If I wer sure they'd bring down things so cheap,
That what mid buy a pound o' mutton now
Would buy the hinder quarters, or the sheep,
Or what wull buy a pig would buy a cow;
In short, if they could meäke a shillèn goo
In market just so vur as two,
Why then, d'ye know, I'd be their man;
But, hang it! I don't think they can.

TOM

Why ees they can, though you don't know't,
An' theäsem men can meäke it clear.
Why vu'st they'd zend up members ev'ry year
To Parli'ment, an' ev'ry man would vote;
Vor if a fellow midden be a squier,
He mid be just so fit to vote, an' goo
To meäke the laws at Lon'on, too,

42

As many that do hold their noses higher.
Why shoulden fellows meäke good laws an' speeches
A-dressed in fusti'n cwoats an' cord'roy breeches?
Or why should hooks an' shovels, zives an' axes,
Keep any man vrom votèn o' the taxes?
An' when the poor've a-got a sheäre
In meäkèn laws, they'll teäke good ceäre
To meäke zome good woones vor the poor.
Do stan' by reason, John; because
The men that be to meäke the laws,
Will meäke em vor theirzelves, you mid be sure.

JOHN

Ees, that they wull. The men that you mid trust
To help you, Tom, would help their own zelves vu'st.

TOM

Aye, aye. But we would have a better plan
O' votèn, than the woone we got. A man,
As things be now, d'ye know, can't goo an' vote
Ageän another man, but he must know't.
We'll have a box an' balls, vor votèn men
To pop their hands 'ithin, d'ye know; an' then,
If woone don't happen vor to lik' a man,
He'll drop a little black ball vrom his han',
An' zend en hwome ageän. He woon't be led
To choose a man to teäke away his bread.

JOHN

But if a man you midden like to 'front,
Should chance to call upon ye, Tom, zome day,
An' ax ye vor your vote, what could ye zay?
Why if you woulden answer, or should grunt
Or bark, he'd know you'd meän 'I won't.'
To promise woone a vote an' not to gi'e 't,
Is but to be a liar an' a cheät.
An' then, bezides, when he did count the balls,

43

An' vind white promises a-turn'd half black;
Why then he'd think the voters all a pack
O' rogues together, – ev'ry woone o'm false.
An' if he had the power, very soon
Perhaps he'd vall upon em, ev'ry woone.
The times be pinchèn me, so well as you,
But I can't tell what ever they can do.

TOM

Why meäke the farmers gi'e their leäbourèn men
Mwore wages, – half or twice so much ageän
As what they got.

JOHN

          But, Thomas, you can't meäke
A man paÿ mwore away than he can teäke.
If you do meäke en gi'e, to till a vield,
So much ageän as what the groun' do yield,
He'll shut out farmèn – or he'll be a goose –
An' goo an' put his money out to use.
Wages be low because the hands be plenty;
They mid be higher if the hands wer skenty.
Leäbour, the seäme's the produce o' the vield,
Do zell at market price – jist what 't 'ill yield.
Thou wouldsten gi'e a zixpence, I do guess,
Vor zix fresh aggs, if zix did zell for less.
If theäsem vo'k could come an' meäke mwore lands,
If they could teäke wold England in their hands
An' stratch it out jist twice so big ageän,
They'd be a-doèn zome'hat vor us then.

TOM

But if they wer a-zent to Parli'ment
To meäke the laws, dost know, as I've a-zaid,
They'd knock the corn-laws on the head;
An' then the landlards must let down their rent,
An' we should very soon have cheaper bread:
Farmers would gi'e less money vor their lands.

JOHN

Aye, zoo they mid, an' prices mid be low'r
Vor what their land would yield; an' zoo their hands
Would be jist where they wer avore.
An' if theäse men wer all to hold together,
They coulden meäke new laws to change the weather!
They ben't so mighty as to think o' frightenèn
The vrost an' raïn, the thunder an' the lightenèn!
An' as vor me, I don't know what to think
O' them there fine, big-talkèn, cunnèn,
Strange men, a-comèn down vrom Lon'on.
Why they don't stint theirzelves, but eat an' drink
The best at public-house where they do staÿ;
They don't work gratis, they do get their paÿ.
They woulden pinch theirzelves to do us good,
Nor gi'e their money vor to buy us food.
D'ye think, if we should meet em in the street
Zome day in Lon'on, they would stand a treat?

TOM

They be a-païd, because they be a-zent
By corn-law vo'k that be the poor man's friends,
To tell us all how we mid gaïn our ends,
A-zendèn peäpers up to Parli'ment.

JOHN

Ah! teäke ccäre how dost trust em. Dost thou know
The funny feäble o' the pig an' crow?
Woone time a crow begun to strut an' hop
About zome groun' that men'd a-been a-drillèn
Wi' barley or zome wheat, in hopes o' villèn
Wi' good fresh corn his empty crop.
But lik' a thief, he didden like the païns
O' workèn hard to get en a vew graïns;
Zoo while the sleeky rogue wer there a-huntèn,
Wi' little luck, vor corns that mid be vound
A-peckèn vor, he heärd a pig a-gruntèn

45

Just tother zide o' hedge, in tother ground.
'Ah!' thought the cunnèn rogue, an' gi'ed a hop,
'Ah! that's the way vor me to vill my crop;
Aye, that's the plan, if nothèn don't defeät it.
If I can get thik pig to bring his snout
In here a bit an' turn the barley out,
Why, hang it! I shall only have to eat it.'
Wi' that he vled up straïght upon a woak,
An' bowèn, lik' a man at hustèns, spoke:
'My friend,' zaid he, 'that's poorish livèn vor ye
In thik there leäze. Why I be very zorry
To zee how they hard-hearted vo'k do sarve ye.
You can't live there. Why! do they meän to starve ye?'
'Ees,' zaid the pig, a-gruntèn, 'ees;
What wi' the hosses an' the geese,
There's only docks an' thissles here to chaw.
Instead o' livèn well on good warm straw,
I got to grub out here, where I can't pick
Enough to meäke me half an ounce o' flick.'
'Well,' zaid the crow, 'd'ye know, if you'll stan' that,
You mussen think, my friend, o' gettèn fat.
D'ye want some better keep? Vor if you do,
Why, as a friend, I be a-come to tell ye,
That if you'll come an' jus' get drough
Theäse gap up here, why you mid vill your belly.
Why, they've a-been a-drillèn corn, d'ye know,
In theäse here piece o' groun' below;
An' if you'll just put in your snout,
An' run en up along a drill,
Why, hang it! you mid grub it out,
An' eat, an' eat your vill.
There idden any feär that vo'k mid come,
Vor all the men be jist a-gone in hwome.'
The pig, believèn ev'ry single word
That wer a-twold en by the cunnèn bird
Wer only vor his good, an' that 'twer true,

Just gi'ed a grunt, an' bundled drough,
An' het his nose, wi' all his might an' maïn,
Right up a drill, a-routèn up the graïn;
An' as the cunnèn crow did gi'e a caw
A-praïsèn o'n, oh! he did veel so proud!
An' work'd, an' blow'd, an' toss'd, an' plough'd
The while the cunnèn crow did vill his maw.
An' after workèn till his bwones
Did eäche, he soon begun to veel
That he should never get a meal,
Unless he dined on dirt an' stwones.
'Well,' zaid the crow, 'why don't ye eat?'
'Eat what, I wonder!' zaid the heäiry plougher,
A-brislèn up an' lookèn rather zour;
'I don't think dirt an' flints be any treat.'
'Well,' zaid the crow, 'why you be blind.
What! don't ye zee how thick the corn do lie
Among the dirt? An' don't ye zee how I
Do pick up all that you do leäve behind?
I'm zorry that your bill should be so snubby.'
'No,' zaid the pig, 'methinks that I do zee
My bill wull do uncommon well vor thee,
Vor thine wull peck, an' mine wull grubby.'
An' just wi' this a-zaid by mister Flick
To mister Crow, wold John the farmer's man
Come up, a-zwingèn in his han'
A good long knotty stick,
An' laid it on, wi' all his might,
The poor pig's vlitches, left an' right;
While mister Crow, that talk'd so fine
O' friendship, left the pig behine,
An' vled away upon a distant tree,
Vor pigs can only grub, but crows can vlee.

Aye, thik there teäle mid do vor children's books;
But you wull vind it hardish for ye
To frighten me, John, wi' a storry
O' silly pigs an' cunnèn rooks.
If we be grubbèn pigs, why then, I s'pose,
The farmers an' the girt woones be the crows.

JOHN

'Tis very odd there idden any friend
To poor-vo'k hereabout, but men mus' come
To do us good away from tother end
Ov England! Han't we any frien's near hwome?
I mus' zay, Thomas, that 'tis rather odd
That strangers should become so very civil,—
That ouer vo'k be children o' the Devil,
An' other vo'k be all the vo'k o' God!
If we've a-got a friend at all,
Why who can tell – I'm sure thou cassen –
But that the squier, or the pa'son,
Mid be our friend, Tom, after all?
The times be hard, 'tis true! an' they that got
His blessèns, shoulden let theirzelves vorget
How 'tis where vo'k do never zet
A bit o' meat within their rusty pot.
The man a-zittèn in his easy chair
To flesh, an' vowl, an' vish, should try to speäre
The poor theäse times, a little vrom his store;
An' if he don't, why sin is at his door.

TOM

Ah! we won't look to that; we'll have our right,—
If not by feäre meäns, then we wull by might.
We'll meäke times better vor us; we'll be free
Ov other vo'k an' others' charity.

JOHN

Ah! I do think you mid as well be quiet;
You'll meäke things wo'se, i'-ma'-be, by a riot.
You'll get into a mess, Tom, I'm afeärd;
You'll goo vor wool, an' then come hwome a-sheär'd.

theäsem, *these*; midden, *might not*; front, *affront*; skenty, *scarce*; chaw, *chew*

My Orcha'd in Linden Lea

'Ithin the woodlands, flow'ry gleäded,
   By the woak tree's mossy moot,
The sheenèn grass-bleädes, timber-sheäded,
   Now do quiver under voot;
An' birds do whissle over head,
An' water's bubblèn in its bed,
An' there vor me the apple tree
Do leän down low in Linden Lea.

When leaves that leätely wer a-springèn
   Now do feäde 'ithin the copse,
An' païnted birds do hush their zingèn
   Up upon the timber's tops;
An' brown-leav'd fruit's a-turnèn red,
In cloudless zunsheen, over head,
Wi' fruit vor me, the apple tree
Do leän down low in Linden Lea.

Let other vo'k meäke money vaster
   In the aïr o' dark-room'd towns,
I don't dread a peevish meäster;
   Though noo man do heed my frowns,
I be free to goo abrode,
Or teäke ageän my hwomeward road
To where, vor me, the apple tree
Do leän down low in Linden Lea.

Ellen Brine ov Allenburn

Noo soul did hear her lips complain,
An' she's a-gone vrom all her païn,
An' others' loss to her is gaïn
Vor she do live in heaven's love;
Vull many a longsome day an' week
She bore her aïlèn, still, an' meek;
A-workèn while her strangth held on,
An' guidèn housework, when 'twer gone.
Vor Ellen Brine ov Allenburn,
Oh! there be souls to murn.

The last time I'd a-cast my zight
Upon her feäce, a-feäded white,
Wer in a zummer's mornèn light
In hall avore the smwold'rèn vier,
The while the children beät the vloor,
In plaÿ, wi' tiny shoes they wore,
An' call'd their mother's eyes to view
The feäts their little limbs could do.
Oh! Ellen Brine ov Allenburn,
They children now mus' murn.

Then woone, a-stoppèn vrom his reäce,
Went up, an' on her knee did pleäce
His hand, a-lookèn in her feäce,
An' wi'a smilèn mouth so small,
He zaid, 'You promised us to goo
To Shroton feäir, an' teäke us two!'
She heärd it wi' her two white ears,
An' in her eyes there sprung two tears,
Vor Ellen Brine ov Allenburn
Did veel that they mus' murn.

September come, wi' Shroton feäir,
But Ellen Brine wer never there!

A heavy heart wer on the meäre
Their father rod his hwomeward road.
'Tis true he brought zome feärèns back,
Vor them two children all in black;
But they had now, wi' plaÿthings new,
Noo mother vor to shew em to,
Vor Ellen Brine ov Allenburn
Would never mwore return.

feärèns, *toys*

Childhood

Aye, at that time our days wer but vew,
An' our lim's wer but small, an' a-growèn;
An' then the feäir worold wer new,
An' life wer all hopevul an' gaÿ;
An' the times o' the sproutèn o' leaves,
An' the cheäk-burnèn seasons o' mowèn,
An' bindèn o' red-headed sheaves,
Wer all welcome seasons o' jaÿ.

Then the housen seem'd high, that be low,
An' the brook did seem wide that is narrow,
An' time, that do vlee, did goo slow,
An' veelèns now feeble wer strong,
An' our worold did end wi' the neämes
Ov the Sha'sbury Hill or Bulbarrow;
An' life did seem only the geämes
That we plaÿ'd as the days rolled along.

Then the rivers, an' high-timber'd lands,
An' the zilvery hills, 'ithout buyèn,
Did seem to come into our hands
Vrom others that own'd em avore;
An' all zickness, an' sorrow, an' need,
Seem'd to die wi' the wold vo'k a-dyèn,
An' leäve us vor ever a-freed
Vrom evils our vorefathers bore.

But happy be children the while
They have elders a-livèn to love em,
An'teäke all the wearisome tweil
That zome hands or others mus' do;
Like the low-headed shrubs that be warm,
In the lewth o' the trees up above em,
A-screen'd vrom the cwold blowèn storm
That the timber avore em must rue.

Meäry's Smile

When mornèn winds, a-blowèn high,
Do zweep the clouds vrom all the sky,
An' laurel-leaves do glitter bright,
The while the newly broken light
Do brighten up, avore our view,
The vields wi' green, an' hills wi' blue;
What then can highten to my eyes
The cheerful feäce ov e'th an' skies,
　　But Meäry's smile, o' Morey's Mill,
　　My rwose o' Mowy Lea.

An' when, at last, the evenèn dews
Do now begin to wet our shoes;
An' night's a-ridèn to the west,
To stop our work, an' gi'e us rest,
Oh! let the candle's ruddy gleäre
But brighten up her sheenèn heäir;
Or else, as she do walk abroad,
Let moonlight show, upon the road,
　　My Meäry's smile, o'Morey's Mill,
　　My rwose o' Mowy Lea.

An' O! mid never tears come on,
To wash her feäce's blushes wan,
Nor kill her smiles that now do plaÿ
Like sparklèn weäves in zunny Maÿ;
But mid she still, vor all she's gone
Vrom souls she now do smile upon,
Show others they can vind woone jaÿ
To turn the hardest work to plaÿ.
　　My Meäry's smile, o' Morey's Mill,
　　My rwose o'Mowy Leá.

Meäry Wedded

The zun can zink, the stars mid rise,
An' woods be green to sheenèn skies;
The cock mid crow to mornèn light,
An' workvo'k zing to vallèn night;
The birds mid whissle on the spraÿ,
An' children leäp in merry plaÿ,
But our's is now a lifeless pleäce,
Vor we've a-lost a smilèn feäce –
  Young Meäry Meäd o' merry mood,
  Vor she's a-woo'd an' wedded.

The dog that woonce wer glad to bear
Her fondlèn vingers down his heäir,
Do leän his head ageän the vloor,
To watch, wi' heavy eyes, the door;
An' men she zent so happy hwome
O' Zadurdays, do seem to come
To door, wi' downcast hearts, to miss
Wi' smiles below the clematis,
  Young Meäry Meäd o' merry mood,
  Vor she's a-woo'd an' wedded.

When they do draw the evenèn blind,
An' when the evenèn light's a-tin'd,
The cheerless vier do drow a gleäre
O'light ageän her empty chair;
An' wordless gaps do now meäke thin
Their talk where woonce her vaïce come in.
Zoo lwonesome is her empty pleäce,
An' blest the house that ha' the feäce
  O' Meäry Meäd o' merry mood,
  Now she's a-woo'd an' wedded.

The day she left her father's he'th,
Though sad, wer kept a day o' me'th,
An' dry-wheel'd waggons' empty beds
Wer left 'ithin the tree-screen'd sheds;
An' all the hosses, at their eäse,
Went snortèn up the flow'ry leäse,
But woone, the smartest vor the roäd,
That pull'd away the dearest lwoad –
    Young Meäry Meäd o' merry mood,
    That wer a-woo'd an' wedded.

a-tin'd, *kindled*; leäse, *unmown field*

The Young that Died in Beauty

If souls should only sheen so bright
In heaven as in e'thly light,
An' nothèn better wer the ceäse,
How comely still, in sheäpe an' feäce,
Would many reach thik happy pleäce,–
The hopevul souls that in their prime
Ha' seem'd a-took avore their time,–
The young that died in beauty.

But when woone's lim's ha'lost their strangth
A-tweilèn drough a lifetime's langth,
An' over cheäks a-growèn wold
The slowly-weästèn years ha' roll'd
The deep'nèn wrinkle's hollow vwold;
When life is ripe, then death do call
Vor less ov thought, than when do vall
On young vo'ks in their beauty.

But pinèn souls, wi'heads a-hung
In heavy sorrow vor the young,
The sister ov the brother dead,
The father wi' a child a-vled,
The husband when his bride ha' laid
Her head at rest, noo mwore to turn,
Have all a-vound the time to murn
Vor youth that died in beauty.

An' yeet the church, where praÿer do rise
Vrom thoughtvul souls, wi' downcast eyes,
An' village greens, a-beät half beäre
By dancers that do meet, an' weär
Such merry looks at feäst an' feäir,
Do gather under leätest skies,
Their bloomèn cheäks an' sparklèn eyes,
Though young ha' died in beauty.

But still the dead shall mwore than keep
The beauty ov their eärly sleep;
Where comely looks shall never weär
Uncomely, under tweil an' ceäre.
The feäir at death be always feäir,
Still feäir to livers' thought an' love,
An' feäirer still to God above,
Than when they died in beauty.

Minden House

'Twer when the vo'k wer out to hawl
A vield o'haÿ a daÿ in June,
An' when the zun begun to vall
Toward the west in afternoon,
Woone only wer a-left behind
To bide indoors, at hwome, an' mind
The house, an' answer vo'k avore
The geäte or door, – young Fanny Deäne.

The aïr 'ithin the geärden wall
Wer deadly still, unless the bee
Did hummy by, or in the hall
The clock did ring a-hettèn dree,
An' there, wi' busy hands, inside
The iron ceäsement, open'd wide,
Did zit an' pull wi' nimble twitch
Her tiny stitch, young Fanny Deäne.

As there she zot she heärd two blows
A-knock'd upon the rumblèn door,
An' laid azide her work, an' rose,
An' walk'd out feäir, athirt the vloor;
An' there, a-holdèn in his hand
His bridled meäre, a youth did stand,
An' mildly twold his neäme and pleäce
Avore the feäce o' Fanny Deäne.

He twold her that he had on hand
Zome business on his father's zide,
But what she didden understand;
An' zoo she ax'd en if he'd ride
Out where her father mid be vound,
Bezide the plow, in Cowslip Ground;
An' there he went, but left his mind
Back there behind, wi' Fanny Deäne.

Ah' oh! his hwomeward road wer gaÿ
In aïr a-blowèn, whiff by whiff,
While sheenèn water-weäves did plaÿ
An' boughs did swaÿ above the cliff;
Vor Time had now a-show'd en dim
The jaÿ it had in store vor him;
An' when he went thik road ageän
His errand then wer Fanny Deäne.

How strangely things be brought about
By Providence, noo tongue can tell.
She minded house, when vo'k wer out,
An' zoo mus' bid the house farewell;
The bees mid hum, the clock mid call
The lwonesome hours 'ithin the hall,
But in behind the woaken door,
There's now noo mwore a Fanny Deäne.

a-hettèn dree, *striking three*

The Wold Wall

Here, Jeäne, we vu'st did meet below
The leafy boughs, a-swingèn slow,
Avore the zun, wi' evenèn glow,
Above our road, a-beamèn red;
The grass in zwath wer in the meäds,
The water gleam'd among the reeds
In aïr a-steälèn roun' the hall,
Where ivy clung upon the wall.
Ah! well-a-day! O wall adieu!
The wall is wold, my grief is new.

An' there you walk'd wi' blushèn pride,
Where softly-wheelèn streams did glide,
Drough sheädes o' poplars at my zide,
An' there wi' love that still do live,
Your feäce did wear the smile o' youth,
The while you spoke wi' age's truth,
An' wi' a rwosebud's mossy ball,
I deck'd your bosom vrom the wall.
Ah! well-a-day! O wall adieu!
The wall is wold, my grief is new.

But now when winter's raïn do vall,
An' wind do beät ageän the hall,
The while upon the wat'ry wall
In spots o' grey the moss do grow,
The ruf noo mwore shall overspread
The pillor ov our weary head,
Nor shall the rwose's mossy ball
Behang vor you the house's wall.
Ah! well-a-day! O wall adieu!
The wall is wold, my grief is new.

Zun-zet

Where the western zun, unclouded,
   Up above the grey hill-tops,
Did sheen drough ashes, lofty sh'ouded,
   On the turf bezide the copse,
     In zummer weather,
     We together,
     Sorrow-slightèn, work-vorgettèn,
     Gambol'd wi' the zun a-zettèn.

There, by flow'ry bows o' bramble,
   Under hedge, in ash-tree sheädes,
The dun-heaïr'd ho'se did slowly ramble
   On the grasses' dewy bleädes,
     Zet free o' lwoads,
     An' stwony rwoads,
     Vorgetvul o' the lashes frettèn,
     Grazèn wi' the zun a-zettèn.

There wer rooks a-beätèn by us
   Drough the aïr, in a vlock,
An' there the lively blackbird, nigh us,
   On the meäple bough did rock,
     Wi' ringèn droat,
     Where zunlight smote
     The yellow boughs o' zunny hedges
     Over western hills' blue edges.

Waters, drough the meäds a-purlèn,
   Glissen'd in the evenèn's light,
An' smoke, above the town a-curlèn,
   Melted slowly out o' zight;
     An' there, in glooms
     Ov unzunn'd rooms,
     To zome, wi' idle sorrows frettèn,
     Zuns did zet avore their zettèn.

We were out in geämes and reäces,
   Loud a-laughèn, wild in me'th,
Wi' windblown heäir, an' zunbrown'd feäces,
   Leäpèn on the high-sky'd e'th,
      Avore the lights
      Wer tin'd o' nights,
      An' while the gossamer's light nettèn
      Sparkled to the zun a-zettèn.

droat, *throat*; me'th, *mirth*

The Water Crowvoot

O small-feäc'd flow'r that now dost bloom
To stud wi' white the shallow Frome,
An' leäve the clote to spread his flow'r
On darksome pools o' stwoneless Stour,
When sof'ly-rizèn aïrs do cool
The water in the sheenèn pool,
Thy beds o' snow-white buds do gleam
So feäir upon the sky-blue stream,
As whitest clouds, a-hangèn high
Avore the blueness o' the sky;
An' there, at hand, the thin-heäir'd cows,
In aïry sheädes o' withy boughs,
Or up bezide the mossy raïls,
Do stan' an' zwing their heavy taïls,
The while the ripplèn stream do flow
Below the dousty bridge's bow;
An' quiv'rèn water-gleams do mock
The weäves, upon the sheäded rock;
An' up athirt the copèn stwone
The laïtren bwoy do leän alwone,
A-watchèn, wi' a stedvast look,
The vallèn waters in the brook,
The while the zand o' time do run
An' leäve his errand still undone.
An' oh! as long's thy buds would gleam
Above the softly-slidèn stream,
While sparklèn zummer-brooks do run
Below the lofty-climèn zun,
I only wish that thou could'st staÿ
Vor noo man's harm, an' all men's jaÿ.

But no, the waterman 'ull weäde
Thy water wi' his deadly bleäde,
To slaÿ thee even in thy bloom,
Fair small-feäc'd flow'r o' the Frome.

laïtren, *loitering*

Trees be Company

When zummer's burnèn het's a-shed
Upon the droopèn grasses head,
A-drevèn under sheädy leaves
The workvo'k in their snow-white sleeves,
We then mid yearn to clim' the height,
    Where thorns be white, above the vern;
An' aïr do turn the zunsheen's might
    To softer light too weak to burn –
        On woodless downs we mid be free,
        But lowland trees be company.

Though downs mid show a wider view
O' green a-reachèn into blue
Than roads a-windèn in the glen,
An' ringèn wi' the sounds o' men;
The thissle's crown o' red an' blue
    In Fall's cwold dew do wither brown,
An' larks come down 'ithin the lew,
    As storms do brew, an' skies do frown –
        An' though the down do let us free,
        The lowland trees be company.

Where birds do zing, below the zun,
In trees above the blue-smok'd tun,
An' sheädes o' stems do overstratch
The mossy path 'ithin the hatch;
If leaves be bright up over head,
    When Maÿ do shed its glitt'rèn light;
Or, in the blight o' Fall, do spread
    A yollow bed avore our zight –
        Whatever season it mid be,
        The trees be always company.

When dusky night do nearly hide
The path along the hedge's zide,
An' daylight's hwomely sounds be still
But sounds o' water at the mill;
Then if noo feäce we long'd to greet
   Could come to meet our lwonesome treäce
Or if noo peäce o' weary veet,
   However fleet, could reach its pleäce –
      However lwonesome we mid be,
      The trees would still be company.

False Friends-like

When I wer still a bwoy, an' mother's pride,
A bigger bwoy spoke up to me so kind-like,
'If you do like, I'll treat ye wi' a ride
In theäse wheel-barrow here.' Zoo I wer blind-like
To what he had a-workèn in his mind-like,
An' mounted vor a passenger inside;
An' comèn to a puddle, perty wide,
He tipp'd me in, a-grinnèn back behind-like.
Zoo when a man do come to me so thick-like,
An' sheäke my hand, where woonce he pass'd me by,
An' tell me he would do me this or that,
I can't help thinkèn o' the big bwoy's trick-like.
An' then, vor all I can but wag my hat
An' thank en, I do veel a little shy.

thick, *friendly*

The Wife a-Lost

Since I noo mwore do zee your feäce,
  Up steäirs or down below,
I'll zit me in the lwonesome pleäce,
  Where flat-bough'd beech do grow;
Below the beeches' bough, my love,
  Where you did never come,
An' I don't look to meet ye now,
  As I do look at hwome.

Since you noo mwore be at my zide,
  In walks in zummer het,
I'll goo alwone where mist do ride,
  Drough trees a-drippèn wet;
Below the raïn-wet bough, my love,
  Where you did never come,
An' I don't grieve to miss ye now,
  As I do grieve at hwome

Since now bezide my dinner-bwoard
  Your vaïce do never sound,
I'll eat the bit I can avword,
  A-vield upon the ground;
Below the darksome bough, my love,
  Where you did never dine,
An' I don't grieve to miss ye now,
  As I at hwome do pine.

Since I do miss your vaïce an' feäce
  In praÿer at eventide,
I'll praÿ wi' woone sad vaïce vor greäce
  To goo where you do bide;
Above the tree an' bough, my love,
  Where you be gone avore,
An' be a-waïtèn vor me now,
  To come vor evermwore.

The Bwoat

Where cows did slowly seek the brink
O' Stour, drough zunburnt grass, to drink;
Wi' vishèn float, that there did zink
    An' rise, I zot as in a dream.
The dazzlèn zun did cast his light
On hedge-row blossom, snowy white,
Though nothèn yet did come in zight,
    A-stirrèn on the straÿen stream;

Till, out by sheädy rocks there show'd,
A bwoat along his foamy road,
Wi' thik feäir maïd at mill, a-row'd
    Wi' Jeäne behind her brother's oars.
An' steätely as a queen o' vo'k,
She zot wi' floatèn scarlet cloak,
An' comèn on, at ev'ry stroke,
    Between my withy-sheäded shores.

The broken stream did idly try
To show her sheäpe a-ridèn by,
The rushes brown-bloom'd stems did ply,
    As if they bow'd to her by will.
The rings o' water, wi' a sock,
Did break upon the mossy rock,
An' gi'e my beätèn heart a shock,
    Above my float's up-leäpèn quill.

Then, lik' a cloud below the skies,
A-drifted off, wi' less'nèn size,
An' lost, she floated vrom my eyes,
    Where down below the stream did wind;

An' left the quiet weäves woonce mwore
To zink to rest, a sky-blue'd vloor,
Wi' all so still's the clote they bore,
   Aye, all but my own ruffled mind.

vo'k, *folk*; sock, *short loud sigh*

Pentridge by the River

Pentridge! – oh! my heart's a-zwellèn
Vull o' jaÿ wi' vo'k a-tellèn
   Any news o' thik wold pleäce,
An' the boughy hedges round it,
An' the river that do bound it
   Wi' his dark but glis'nèn feäce.
Vor there's noo land, on either hand,
To me lik' Pentridge by the river.

Be there any leaves to quiver
On the aspen by the river?
   Doo he sheäde the water still,
Where the rushes be a-growèn,
Where the sullen Stour's a-flowèn
   Drough the meäds vrom mill to mill?
Vor if a tree wer dear to me,
Oh! 'twer thik aspen by the river.

There, in eegrass new a-shootèn,
I did run on even vootèn,
   Happy, over new-mow'd land;
Or did zing wi' zingèn drushes
While I plaïted, out o' rushes,
   Little baskets vor my hand;
Bezide the clote that there did float,
Wi' yollow blossoms, on the river.

When the western zun's a-vallèn,
What sh'ill vaïce is now a-callèn
   Hwome the deäiry to the païls;
Who do dreve em on, a-flingèn
Wide-bow'd horns, or slowly zwingèn
   Right an' left their tufty taïls?
As they do goo a-huddled drough
The geäte a-leädèn up vrom river.

Bleäded grass is now a-shootèn
Where the vloor wer woonce our vootèn,
   While the hall wer still in pleäce.
Stwones be looser in the wallèn;
Hollow trees be nearer vallèn;
   Ev'ry thing ha' chang'd its feäce.
But still the neäme do bide the seäme –
'Tis Pentridge – Pentridge by the river.

drushes, *thrushes*

My Love's Guardian Angel

As in the cool-aïr'd road I come by,
                            – in the night,
Under the moon-clim'd height o' the sky,
                            – in the night,
There by the lime's broad lim's as I staÿ'd,
Dark in the moonlight, bough's sheädows plaÿ'd
Up on the window-glass that did keep
Lew vrom the wind, my true love asleep,
                            – in the night.
While in the grey-wall'd height o' the tow'r,
                            – in the night,
Sounded the midnight bell wi' the hour,
                            – in the night,
There lo! a bright-heäir'd angel that shed
Light vrom her white robe's zilvery thread,
Put her vore-vinger up vor to meäke
Silence around lest sleepers mid weäke,
                            – in the night.

'Oh! then,' I whisper'd, 'do I behold
                            – in the night,
Linda, my true-love, here in the cwold,
                            – in the night?'
'No,' she meäde answer, 'you do misteäke:
She is asleep, but I that do weäke,
Here be on watch, an angel a-blest,
Over her slumber while she do rest,
                            – in the night.

'Zee how the winds, while here by the bough,
                            – in the night,
They do pass on, don't smite on her brow,
                            – in the night;
Zee how the cloud-sheädes naïseless do zweep

74

Over the house-top where she's asleep.
You, too, goo by, in times that be near,
You too, as I, mid speak in her ear
                              – in the night.'

The Lark

As I, below the mornèn sky,
   Wer out a-workèn in the lew
O' black-stemm'd thorns, a-springèn high,
   Avore the worold-boundèn blue,
A-reäkèn, under woak tree boughs,
The orts a-left behin' by cows.

Above the grey-grow'd thistle rings,
   An' deäisy-buds, the lark, in flight,
Did zing aloft, wi' flappèn wings,
   Tho' mwore in heärèn than in zight;
The while my bwoys, in playvul me'th,
Did run till they wer out o' breath.

Then woone, wi' han'-besheäded eyes,
   A-stoppèn still, as he did run,
Look'd up to zee the lark arise
   A-zingèn to the high-gone zun;
The while his brother look'd below
Vor what the groun' mid have to show.

Zoo woone did watch above his head
   The bird his hands could never teäke;
An' woone, below, where he did tread,
   Vound out the nest within the breäke;
But, aggs be only woonce a-vound,
An' uncaught larks ageän mid sound.

orts, *loose hay put out for cows*

Woak Hill

When sycamore leaves wer a-spreadèn,
   Green-ruddy, in hedges,
Bezide the red doust o' the ridges,
   A-dried at Woak Hill;

I packed up my goods all a-sheenèn
   Wi' long years o' handlèn,
On dousty red wheels ov a waggon,
   To ride at Woak Hill.

The brown thatchen ruf o' the dwellèn
   I then wer a-leävèn,
Had shelter'd the sleek head o' Meäry,
   My bride at Woak Hill.

But now vor zome years, her light voot-vall
   'S a-lost vrom the vloorèn.
Too soon vor my jaÿ an' my children,
   She died at Woak Hill.

But still I do think that, in soul,
   She do hover about us;
To ho vor her motherless children,
   Her pride at Woak Hill.

Zoo – lest she should tell me hereafter
   I stole off'ithout her,
An' left her, uncall'd at house-riddèn,
   To bide at Woak Hill–

I call'd her so fondly, wi' lippèns
   All soundless to others,
An' took her wi' aïr-reachèn hand,
   To my zide at Woak Hill.

On the road I did look round, a-talkèn
   To light at my shoulder,

An' then led her in at the door-way,
   Miles wide vrom Woak Hill.

An' that's why vo'k thought, vor a season,
   My mind wer a-wandrèn
Wi' sorrow, when I wer so sorely
   A-tried at Woak Hill.

But no; that my Meäry mid never
   Behold herzelf slighted,
I wanted to think that I guided
   My guide vrom Woak Hill.

ho, *care*

Pickèn o' Scroff

Oh! the wood wer a-vell'd in the copse,
   An' the moss-bedded primrwose did blow;
An' vrom tall-stemmèd trees' leafless tops,
   There did lie but slight sheädes down below.
An' the sky wer a-showèn, in drough
By the tree-stems, the deepest o' blue,
Wi' a light that did vall on an' off
The dry ground, a-strew'd over wi' scroff.

There the hedge that were leätely so high,
   Wer a-plush'd, an' along by the zide,
Where the waggon 'd a-haul'd the wood by,
   There did reach the deep wheelrouts, a-dried.
An' the groun' wi' the sticks wer bespread,
Zome a-cut off alive, an' zome dead,
An' vor burnèn, well wo'th reäkèn off,
By the children a-pickèn o' scroff.

In the tree-studded leäze, where the woak
   Wer a-spreadèn his head out around,
There the scrags that the wind had a-broke,
   Wer a-lyèn about on the ground,
Or the childern, wi' little red hands,
Wer a-tyèn em up in their bands;
Vor noo squier or farmer turn'd off
Little childern a-pickèn o' scroff.

There wer woone bloomèn child wi' a cloak
   On her shoulders, as green as the ground;
An' another, as gray as the woak,
   Wi' a bwoy in a brown frock, a-brown'd.
An woone got up, in plaÿ, vor to taït,
On a woak-limb, a-growèn out straïght.
But she soon wer a-taïted down off,
By her meätes out a-pickèn o' scroff.

When they childern do grow to staïd vo'k,
    An' goo out in the worold, all wide
Vrom the copse, an' the zummerleäze woak,
    Where at last all their elders ha' died,
They wull then vind it touchèn to bring,
To their minds, the sweet springs o' their spring,
Back avore the new vo'k did turn off
The poor childern a-pickèn o' scroff.

Scroff, *bits of wood, windfalls*; scrags, *crooked tree branches*; taït, *play see-
saw*

The Rwose in the Dark

In zummer, leäte at evenèn tide,
    I zot to spend a moonless hour
'Ithin the window, wi' the zide
    A-bound wi' rwoses out in flow'r,
Bezide the bow'r, vorsook o' birds,
An' listen'd to my true-love's words.

A-risèn to her comely height,
    She push'd the swingèn ceäsement round;
And I could hear, beyond my zight,
    The win'-blow'd beech-tree softly sound,
On higher ground, a-swäyèn slow,
On drough my happy hour below.

An' tho' the darkness then did hide
    The dewy rwose's blushèn bloom,
He still did cast sweet aïr inside
    To Jeäne, a-chattèn in the room;
An' though the gloom did hide her feäce,
Her words did bind me to the pleäce.

An' there, while she, wi' runnèn tongue,
    Did talk unzeen 'ithin the hall,
I thought her like the rwose that flung
    His sweetness vrom his darken'd ball,
'Ithout the wall, an' sweet's the zight
Ov her bright feäce by mornèn light.

The Child an' the Mowers

O, aye! they had woone child bezide,
    An' a finer your eyes never met,
'Twer a dear little fellow that died
    In the zummer that come wi' such het;
By the mowers, too thoughtless in fun,
    He wer then a-zent off vrom our eyes,
Vrom the light ov the dew-dryèn zun,—
    Aye! vrom days under blue-hollow'd skies.

He went out to the mowers in meäd,
    When the zun wer a-rose to his height,
An' the men wer a-swingèn the sneäd,
    Wi' their eärms in white sleeves, left an' right;
An' out there, as they rested at noon,
    O! they drench'd en vrom eäle-horns too deep,
Till his thoughts wer a-drown'd in a swoon;
    Aye! his life wer a-smother'd in sleep.

Then they laid en there-right on the ground,
    On a grass-heap, a-zweltrèn wi' het,
Wi' his heäir all a-wetted around
    His young feäce, wi' the big drops o' zweat;
In his little left palm he'd a-zet,
    Wi' his right hand, his vore-vinger's tip,
As vor zome'hat he woulden vorget,—
    Aye! zome thought that he woulden let slip.

Then they took en in hwome to his bed,
    An' he rose vrom his pillow noo mwore,
Vor the curls on his sleek little head
    To be blown by the wind out o' door.

Vor he died while the haÿ russled grey
   On the staddle so leätely begun:
Lik' the mown-grass a-dried by the day,–
   Aye! the zwath-flow'r's a-killed by the zun.

sneäd, *scythe stem*; staddle, *footings of a rick*

The Turnstile

Ah! sad wer we as we did peäce
The wold church road, wi' downcast feäce,
The while the bells, that mwoan'd so deep
Above our child a-left asleep,
Wer now a-zingén all alive
Wi' tother bells to meäke the vive.
But up at woone pleäce we come by,
'Twer hard to keep woone's two eyes dry;
On Steän-cliff road, 'ithin the drong,
Up where, as vo'k do pass along,
The turnèn stile, a-païnted white,
Do sheen by day an' show by night.
Vor always there, as we did goo
To church, thik stile did let us drough,
Wi' spreadèn eärms that wheel'd to guide
Us each in turn to tother zide.
An' vu'st ov all the traïn he took
My wife, wi' winsome gäit an' look;
An' then zent on my little maïd,
A-skippèn onward, overjaÿ'd
To reach ageän the pleäce o' pride,
Her comely mother's left han' zide.
An' then, a-wheelèn roun', he took
On me, 'ithin his third white nook.
An' in the fourth, a-sheäkèn wild,
He zent us on our giddy child.
But eesterday he guided slow
My downcast Jenny, vull o' woe,
An' then my little maïd in black,
A-walkèn softly on her track;

An' after he'd a-turn'd ageän,
To let me goo along the leäne,
He had noo little bwoy to vill
His last white eärms, an' they stood still.

vive, *five*

Which Road?

Still green on the limbs o' the woak wer the leaves,
Where the black slooe did grow, a-meal'd over wi'grey,
Though leäzes, a-burnt, wer wi' bennets a-brown'd,
An' the stubble o' wheat wer a-witherèn white,
While sooner the zunlight did zink vrom the zight,
An' longer did linger the dim-roaded night.

But bright wer the day-light a-dryèn the dew,
As foam wer a-villèn the pool in its vall,
An' a-sheenèn did climb, by the chalk o' the cliff,
The white road a-voun' steep to the wayweary step,
Where along by the knap, wi' a high-beätèn breast,
Went the maïd an' the chap to the feäst in their best.

There hosses went by wi' their neck in a bow,
An' did toss up their nose, over outspringén knees;
An' the ox, heäiryhided, wi' low-swingén head;
An' the sheep, little knee'd, wi' a quick-dippèn nod;
An' a maïd, wi' her head a-borne on, in a proud
Gaït o' walkèn, so smooth as an aïr-zwimmèn cloud.

bennets, *stalks of grass*

Jaÿ a-Pass'd

When leaves, in evenèn winds, do vlee,
Where mornèn aïr did strip the tree,
The mind can waït vor boughs in spring
To cool the elem-sheäded ring.
Where orcha'd blooth's white sceäles do vall
Mid come the apple's blushèn ball.
Our hopes be new, as time do goo,
A-measur'd by the zun on high,
Avore our jaÿs do pass us by.

When ice did melt below the zun,
An' weäves along the streäm did run,
I hoped in Maÿ's bright froth to roll,
Lik' jess'my in a lily's bowl.
Or, if I lost my loose-bow'd swing,
My wrigglèn kite mid pull my string,
An' when noo ball did rise an' vall,
Zome other geäme wud still be nigh,
Avore my jaÿs all pass'd me by.

I look'd, as childhood pass'd along,
To walk, in leäter years, man-strong,
An' look'd ageän, in manhood's pride,
To manhood's sweetest chaïce, a bride:
An' then to childern, that mid come
To meäke my house a dearer hwome.
But now my mind do look behind
Vor jaÿs; an' wonder, wi' a sigh,
When 'twer my jaÿs all pass'd me by.

Wer it when, woonce, I miss'd a call
To rise, an' seem'd to have a vall?
Or when my Jeäne to my hands left
Her vew bright keys, a dolevul heft?

Or when avore the door I stood,
To watch a child a-gone vor good?
Or where zome crowd did laugh aloud;
Or when the leaves did spring, or die?
When did my jaÿ all pass me by?

jess'my, *cuckoo orchid*; heft, *weight*

Aïr an' Light

Ah! look an' zee how widely free
To all the land the win' do goo;
If here a tree do swaÿ, a tree
On yon'er hill's a-swaÿen too.
How wide the light do bring to zight
The pleäce an' liven feäce o' man;
How vur the stream do run vor lip
To drink, or hand to sink and dip!

But oone mid be a-smote wi' woe
That middèn pass, in wider flight,
To other souls, a-droopèn low,
An' hush'd like birds at vall o' night.
But zome be sad wi' others glad;
In turn we all mid murn our lot,
An' many a day that have a-broke
Oone heart is jaÿ to other vo'k.

The mornèn zun do cast abroad
His light on drops o' dewy wet,
An' down below his noontide road
The streams do gleäre below his het;
His evenèn light do sparkle bright
Across the quiv'rèn gossamer;
But I, though fair he still mid glow,
Do miss a zight he cannot show.

The Vierzide Chairs

Though days do gaïn upon the night,
An' birds do teäke a leäter flight,
'Tis cwold enough to spread our hands
Oonce now an' then to glowèn brands.
Zoo now we two, a-left alwone,
Can meäke a quiet hour our own,
Let's teäke, a-zittèn feäce to feäce,
Our pleäces by the vier pleäce,
Where you shall have the window view
Outside, an' I can look on you.

When oonce I brought ye hwome my bride,
In yollow glow o' zummer tide,
I wanted you to teäke a chair
At that zide o' the vier, there,
And have the ground an' sky in zight
Wi' feäce toward the window light;
While I back here should have my brow
In sheäde, an' zit where I do now,
That you mid zee the land outside,
If I could look on you, my bride.

An' there the water-pool do spread,
Wi' swayèn elems over head,
An' there's the knap where we did rove
At dusk, along the high-tree'd grove,
The while the wind did whisper down
Our whisper'd words; an' there's the crown
Ov Duncliffe hill, wi' wid'nèn sheädes
Ov wood a-cast on slopèn gleädes:
Zoo you injoy the green an' blue
Without, an' I will look on you.

An' there's the copse, where we did all
Goo out-a-nuttèn in the fall,

That now would meäke, a-quiv'rèn black,
But little lewth behind your back;
An' there's the tower, near the door,
That we at dusk did meet avore
As we did gather on the green,
An' you did zee, an' wer a-zeen:
All wold zights welcomer than new,
A-look'd on as I look'd on you.

The Stwonen Steps

Theäse stwonen steps a-zet so true
Wi' top on top, a voot each wide,
Did always clim' the slopèn zide
O' theäse steep ledge, vor me an' you.
Had men a-built the steps avore
The mossy arch ov our wold door?
Wer theäse wold steäirs a-laid by man
Avore the bridge's archèd span?
Had vo'k a-put the stwones down here
Avore they piled the church's speer?
Ah! who do know how long agoo
The steps vu'st bore a shoe?

An' here bezide the slopèn hump,
Vrom stwone to stwone, a-lyèn flat,
The children's little veet do pat,
An' men-vo'k's heavy zoles do clump.
Ah! which the last shall beät a shoe
On theäse grey stwones: shall I or you?
Which little boy o' mine shall clim'
The steps the last, my John or Jim?
Which maïd, child-quick or woman-slow,
Shall walk the last theäse stwones in row?
Who can ever tell us who
The last shall come or goo?

The road do leäd below the blocks
To yonder springhead's stwonen cove,
An' Squier's house, an elem grove,
An' mill bezide the foamy rocks.
An' aye, theäse well-wore blocks o' stwone
Wer here when I vu'st run alwone;
The stwonèn steäirs wer here avore
My father put a voot to vloor.

'Twer up the steps that gramfer come
To court poor grammer at her hwome.
But who can ever tell what peäirs
O' veet trod vu'st the steäirs?

grammer, *grandmother*

The Vield Path

Here oonce did sound sweet words, a-spoke
   In wind that swum
   Where ivy clomb,
About the ribby woak;
An' still the words, though now a-gone,
Be dear to me, that linger on.

An' here, as comely vo'k did pass,
   Their sheädes did slide
   Below their zide,
Along the flow'ry grass,
An' though the sheädes be all a-gone,
Still dear's the ground they vell upon.

But could they come where then they stroll'd,
   However young
   Mid sound their tongue,
Their sheädes would show em wold;
But dear, though they be all a-gone,
Be sheädes o' trees that linger on.

O ashèn poles, a-sheenèn tall!
   You be too young
   To have a-sprung
In days when I wer small;
But you, broad woak, wi' ribby rind,
Wer here so long as I can mind.

The Wind at the Door

As day did darken on the dewless grass,
    There still, wi' nwone a-come by me,
    To staÿ awhile at hwome by me,
    Within the house, all dumb by me,
I zot me sad as evenèntide did pass.

An' there a win'-blast shook the rattlèn door,
    An' seem'd, as win' did mwoan without,
    As if my Jeäne, alwone without,
    A-stannèn on the stwone without,
Wer there a-come wi' happiness oonce mwore.

I went to door; an' out vrom trees above
    My head, upon the blast by me,
    Sweet blossoms wer a-cast by me,
    As if my love, a-past by me,
Did fling em down – a token ov her love.

'Sweet blossoms o' the tree where I do murn,'
    I thought, 'if you did blow vor her,
    Vor apples that should grow vor her,
    A-vallèn down below vor her,
O then how happy I should zee you kern.'

But no. Too soon I voun' my charm a-broke.
    Noo comely soul in white like her –
    Noo soul a-steppèn light like her –
    An' nwone o' comely height like her –
Went by; but all my grief ageän awoke.

kern, *grow into fruit*

Melhill Feast

Aye there, at the feäst by Melhill's brow,
So softly below the clouds in flight,
Did glide on the wood the sheäde an' light,
Tree after tree, an' bough by bough.

An' there, as among the crowd I took
My wanderèn way, bwoth to an' fro,
Vull comely wer sheäpes the day did show,
Feäce upon feäce, an' look by look.

An' there, among maïdens left an' right,
On oone o' the feäirest I did zet
My looks all the mwore the mwore we met,
Glance upon glance, an' zight by zight.

The way she'd a-come by then wer soon
The happiest road that I did goo,
By glitterèn gossamer or dew,
Evenèn by evenèn, moon by moon.

Along by the doors o' maïdens feäir,
As feäir as the best till she is nigh,
Though now I can heedless pass em by,
Oone after oone, or peäir by peäir.

Vust by the orcha'ds dim an' cool,
An' then along Woodcombe's timber'd zide,
Then by the meäds, where streäms do glide,
Shallow by shallow, pool by pool.

An' then to the house, a-zet alwone,
Wi' rwoses a-hung on pworch an' wall,
Where up by the bridge the stream do vall,
Rock under rock, an' stwone by stwone.

Sweet wer the hopes that then did cheer
My heart as I thought on times to come,
Wi' her vor to bless my happy hwome,
Moon upon moon, an' year by year.

White an' Blue

My love is o' comely height, an' straïght,
An' comely in all her ways an' gaït;
In feäce she do show the rwose's hue,
An' her lids on her eyes be white on blue.

When Elemley clubmen walk'd in Maÿ
An' vo'k come in clusters, ev'ry waÿ,
As soon as the zun dried up the dew,
An' clouds in the sky wer white on blue,

She come by the down, wi' trippèn walk,
By deäisies, an' sheenèn banks o' chalk,
An' brooks, where the crowvoot flow'rs did strew
The sky-tinted water, white on blue.

She nodded her head, as plaÿ'd the band;
She dapp'd wi' her voot, as she did stand;
She danced in a reel, a-wearèn new
A skirt wi' a jacket, white wi' blue.

I singled her out vrom thin an' stout,
Vrom slender an' stout I chose her out;
An' what, in the evenèn, could I do,
But gi'e her my breast-knot, white an' blue?

clubmen, *morris dancers*

The Geäte a-Vallèn to

In the zunsheen ov our zummers
   Wi' the haÿ time now a-come,
How busy wer we out a-vield
   Wi' vew a-left at hwome,
When waggons rumbled out ov yard
   Red wheeled, wi' body blue,
As back behind 'em loudly slamm'd
   The geäte a-vallèn to.

Drough daÿsheen ov how many years
   The geäte ha' now a-swung
Behind the veet o' vull-grown men
   An' vootsteps ov the young.
Drough years o' days it swung to us
   Behind each little shoe,
As we tripped lightly on avore
   The geäte a-vallèn to.

In evenèn time o' starry night
   How mother zot at hwome,
An' kept her bleäzèn vire bright
   Till father should ha' come,
An' how she quicken'd up an' smiled
   An' stirred her vire anew,
To hear the trampèn ho'ses' steps
   An' geäte a-vallèn to.

There's moon-sheen now in nights o' fall
   When leaves be brown vrom green,
When, to the slammèn o' the geäte,
   Our Jenny's ears be keen,
When the wold dog do wag his taïl,
   An' Jeän could tell to who,
As he do come in drough the geäte,
   The geäte a-vallèn to.

An' oft do come a saddened hour
    When there must goo away
One well-beloved to our heart's core,
    Vor long, perhaps vor aye:
An' oh! it is a touchèn thing
    The lovèn heart must rue,
To hear behind his last farewell
    The geäte a-vallèn to.

Rustic Childhood

No city primness train'd our feet
To strut in childhood through the street,
But freedom let them loose to tread
The yellow cowslip's downcast head;
Or climb, above the twining hop
And ivy, to the elm-tree's top;
Where southern airs of blue-sky'd day
Breath'd o'er the daisy and the may.
    I knew you young, and love you now,
     O shining grass, and shady bough.

Far off from town, where splendour tries
To draw the looks of gather'd eyes,
And clocks, unheeded, fail to warn
The loud-tongued party of the morn,
We spent in woodland shades our day
In cheerful work or happy play,
And slept at night where rustling leaves
Threw moonlight shadows o'er our eaves.
    I knew you young, and love you now,
     O shining grass, and shady bough.

Or in the grassy drove by ranks
Of white-stemm'd ashes, or by banks
Of narrow lanes, in-winding round
The hedgy sides of shelving ground;
Where low-shot light struck in to end
Again at some cool-shaded bend,
Where we might see through darkleav'd boughs
The evening light on green hill-brows.
    I knew you young, and love you now,
     O shining grass, and shady bough.

Or on the hillock where we lay
At rest on some bright holyday;
When short noon-shadows lay below
The thorn in blossom white as snow;
And warm air bent the glist'ning tops
Of bushes in the lowland copse,
Before the blue hills swelling high
And far against the southern sky.
     I knew you young, and love you now,
     O shining grass, and shady bough.

The Eegrass

With stricken heart, and melting mood,
I rov'd along the mead to brood
In freedom, at the eventide,
On souls that time has scatter'd wide;
As by the boughy hedge's side
   The shadows darken'd into night,
   And cooling airs, with wanton flight,
      Were blowing o'er the eegrass.

There fancy roam'd from place to place,
From year to year, to find some face
That I no more shall look upon,
Or see in sadness, sorrow-wan,
Or time-worn with its brightness gone;
   And my own Lucy, fair to see,
   Seem'd there to come again to me,
      Up o'er the shining eegrass.

As when upon a summer's day,
While we were there at hawling hay,
With downcast look she lightly drew
Her rake-head to her shapely shoe,
With hands well skill'd to bring it through
   The tangled crowfoot-stems, that broke
   The rakes for us poor clumsy folk,
      And still are in the eegrass.

And there the storms that spring clouds shed
Fell lately on her hooded head,
The while she sat, at eventide,
A-milking by her dun cow's side;
And there, when summer, sunny-skied
   And boughy-wooded, brought its heat,
   She trod the flow'rs with light-shod feet,
      But comes not o'er the eegrass.

O summer all thy crops are down,
And copse and leaze are turning brown,
And cuckoos leave the boughs to fade
Through waning fall, within the glade;
And we have lost our blooming maid.
  So all thou broughtest fresh and fair
  Begins to wither ev'ry where,
    But this bright-bladed eegrass.

Moss

O rain-bred moss that now dost hide
The timber's bark and wet rock's side,
Upshining to the sun, between
The darksome storms, in lively green,
And wash'd by pearly rain drops clean,
  Steal o'er my lonely path, and climb
  My wall, dear child of silent time.
    O winter moss, creep on, creep on,
    And warn me of the time that's gone.

Green child of winter, born to take
Whate'er the hands of man forsake,
That makest dull, in rainy air,
His labour-brighten'd works; so fair
While newly left in summer's glare;
  And stealest o'er the stone that keeps
  His name in mem'ry where he sleeps.
    O winter moss, creep on, creep on,
    And warn us of the time that's gone.

Come lowly plant that lov'st, like me,
The shadow of the woodland tree,
And waterfall where echo mocks
The milkmaid's song by dripping rocks,
And sunny turf for roving flocks,
  And ribby elms extending wide
  Their roots within the hillock's side.
    Come winter moss, creep on, creep on,
    And warn me of the time that's gone.

Come, meet me wandering, and call
My mind to some green mould'ring hall
That once stood high, the fair-wall'd pride
Of hearts that lov'd, and hoped, and died,

Ere thou hadst climb'd around its side:
　　Where blooming faces once were gay
　　For eyes no more to know the day.
　　　　Come winter moss, creep on, creep on,
　　　　And warn me of the time that's gone.

While there in youth, – the sweetest part
Of life, – with joy-believing heart,
They liv'd their own dear days, all fraught
With incidents for after-thought
In later life, when fancy brought
　　The outline of some faded face
　　Again to its forsaken place.
　　　　Come winter moss, creep on, creep on,
　　　　And warn me of the time that's gone.

Come where thou climbedst, fresh and free,
The grass-beglooming apple-tree,
That, hardly shaken with my small
Boy's strength, with quiv'ring head, let fall
The apples we lik'd most of all,
　　Or elm I climb'd, with clasping legs,
　　To reach the crow's high-nested eggs.
　　　　Come winter moss, creep on, creep on,
　　　　And warn me of the time that's gone.

Or where I found thy yellow bed
Below the hill-borne fir-tree's head,
And heard the whistling east wind blow
Above, while wood-screen'd down below
I rambled in the spring-day's glow,
　　And watch'd the low-ear'd hares upspring
　　From cover, and the birds take wing.
　　　　Come winter moss, creep on, creep on,
　　　　And warn me of the time that's gone.

Or where the bluebells bent their tops
In windless shadows of the copse;

Or where the misty west wind blew
O'er primroses that peer'd out through
Thy bankside bed, and scatter'd dew
    O'er grey spring grass I watch'd alone
    Where thou hadst grown o'er some old stone.
        Come winter moss, creep on, creep on,
        And warn me of the time that's gone.

Plorata Veris Lachrymis

O now, my true and dearest bride,
Since thou hast left my lonely side,
My life has lost its hope and zest.
The sun rolls on from east to west,
But brings no more that evening rest,
Thy loving-kindness made so sweet,
And time is slow that once was fleet,
     As day by day was waning.

The last sad day that show'd thee lain
Before me, smiling in thy pain,
The sun soar'd high along his way
To mark the longest summer day,
And show to me the latest play
Of thy sweet smile, and thence, as all
The daylengths shrunk from small to small,
     My joy began its waning.

And now 'tis keenest pain to see
Whate'er I saw in bliss with thee.
The softest airs that ever blow,
The fairest days that ever glow,
Unfelt by thee, but bring me woe.
And sorrowful I kneel in pray'r,
Which thou no longer, now, canst share,
     As day by day is waning.

How can I live my lonesome days?
How can I tread my lonesome ways?
How can I take my lonesome meal?
Or how outlive the grief I feel?
Or how again look on to weal?
Or sit, at rest, before the heat
Of winter fires, to miss thy feet,
     When evening light is waning?

Thy voice is still I lov'd to hear,
Thy voice is lost I held so dear.
Since death unlocks thy hand from mine,
No love awaits me such as thine.
Oh! boon the hardest to resign!
But if we meet again at last
In heav'n, I little care how fast
    My life may now be waning.

My Dearest Julia

Oh! can or can I not live on,
Forgetting thee, my love forgone?
'Tis true, where joyful faces crowd
And merry tongues are ringing loud,
Or where some needful work unwrought
May call for all my care and thought,
Or where some landscape, bath'd in light,
May spread to fascinate my sight,
Thy form may melt awhile, as fade
Our shades within some welkin shade,
    And I awhile may then live on,
    Forgetting thee, my love forgone.

But then the thrilling thought comes on,
    Of all thy love that's now forgone;
Thy daily toil to earn me wealth,
Thy grief to see me out of health,
Thy yearning readiness to share
The burden of my toil and care,
And all the blessings thou hast wrought
In my behalf by deed and thought.
And then I seem to hear thee calling,
Gloomy fac'd with tear drops falling,
    'Canst thou then so soon live on,
    Forgetful of my love forgone?'

The River Stour

Stour, of all our streams the dearest
Unto me, for thou was nearest
  To my boyhood in my play,
Blest may be the sons and daughters
That beside thy wand'ring waters
  Have their hearth, and spend their day.
By happy homes of high and low
Flow on dark river, ever flow.

Thou through meady Blackmore wendest,
And around its hillslopes bendest,
  Under cliffs, and down the dells;
On by uplands under tillage,
On beside the tower'd village,
  With its sweetly-chiming bells.
There go, dear stream, and ever flow
By souls, in joy, without a woe.

Wind around the woody ridges;
Shoot below thy archy bridges,
  Swelling by thy many brooks;
Gliding slowly in thy deepness;
Rolling fleetly at thy steepness;
  Whirling round the shady nooks;
And pass the lands that fall and rise
Below the sight of tearless eyes,

Where the willow's head begloometh
Depths below the clote, that bloometh
  Near the rushes' brown-clubb'd wand,
While to mill by mill thou roamest,
And below the mill-weir foamest
  In the wildly-heaving pond.
And when, at night, the wheel may cease
To roll, may inmates sleep in peace.

Where a hoof or foot onspeedeth
By a well-stein'd road, that leadeth
    O'er thy face to either side,
To the town, that's many-streeted,
Where, by loving friends, are greeted
    Friend and child, and maid and bride,
May their welfare ne'er give out
Until thy stream is dried by drought.

Glowing under day's warm sunning,
Sparkling with thy ripples' running,
    Taking to thee brooks and rills,
Valley-draining, dell-bewending,
Water-taking, water-sending,
    Down to dairy farms and mills,
O blest below each village tow'r
Be thy by-dwellers, gliding Stour.

The Moor

Where yonder leaning hill-side roves
　　With woody dippings, far around,
And many jutting brows, and coves,
　　Of rugged cliffs, and slopy ground,
Beside the stream that slowly sinks
　　With reaches tinted from the skies,
　　And stream-side meadows, lowly lies
The moor, with dikes and sedgy brinks.

About us there the willow shade
　　Oft play'd beside the water's edge,
And there the rodded bulrush sway'd
　　Its soft brown club, above the sedge,
And by the aspen or the bridge,
　　The angler sat, and lightly whipp'd
　　His little float, that, dancing, dipp'd
From o'er the waveling's little ridge.

There cows, in clusters, rambled wide,
　　Some hanging low their heads to eat,
Some lying on their heavy side,
　　Some standing on their two-peaked feet,
Some sheeted white, some dun or black,
　　Some red, and others brindled dark,
　　Some marked with milk-white star, or spark,
And ours all white along the back.

There cows, to others, low'd; now here,
　　Now there, from open heat to shade;
And out among them, far or near,
　　With quiv'ring scream, the horses neigh'd,

The while some boy, within the mead,
   On some high mare might come astride;
   And sliding down her bulging side,
Might set her, snorting, free to feed.

And there we saw the busy crow
   For mussels down the river play,
And rooks sweep on where men below
   Went, water hemm'd, their crooked way,
And gamb'ling boys, in merry train,
   On holidays came rambling by
   With often-grounded poles, to fly
In high-bow'd flight, o'er dike and drain.

There men at work on pathless grass,
   Are seen, though out of hearing, wide,
By neighbour-meeting folk, that pass
   The many-roaded upland side.
So some may like the trampled road,
   O'er well-rubbed stile-bars, with a gloss,
   And some the moor, that some may cross
But pass no door of man's abode.

Seasons and Times

Awhile in the dead of the winter,
The wind hurries keen through the sunshine,
But finds no more leaves that may linger
On tree-boughs to strew on the ground.

Long streaks of bright snow-drift, bank-shaded,
Yet lie on the slopes, under hedges;
But still all the road out to Thorndon
Would not wet a shoe on the ground.

The days, though the cold seems to strengthen,
Outlengthen their span, and the evening
Seeks later and later its westing,
To cast its dim hue on the ground,

'Till tree-heads shall thicken their shadow
With leaves of a glittering greenness,
And daisies shall fold up their blossoms
At evening, in dew on the ground;

And then, in the plum-warding garden,
Or shadowy orchard, the house-man
Shall smile at his fruit, really blushing,
Where sunheat shoots through on the ground.

What season do you feel the fairest –
The season of sowing or growing,
Or season of mowing and ripeness,
When hay may lie new on the ground?

And like you the glittering morning,
Or short-shaded noon, or the coming
Of slant-lighted evening, or moonlight,
When footsteps are few on the ground?